POET

LUIS DE GÓNGORA
Selected Shorter Poems

LUIS DE GÓNGORA

Selected Shorter Poems

VERSIONS BY
MICHAEL SMITH

Anvil Press Poetry

Published in 1995
by Anvil Press Poetry Ltd
69 King George Street London SE10 8PX

Copyright © Michael Smith 1995

This book is published
with financial assistance from
The Arts Council of England

This translation has been made
with the support of the Dirección General
del Libro y Bibliotecas
del Ministerio de Cultura de España

Designed and composed by Anvil
Photoset in Palatino by Typestream
Printed at Alden Press Limited
Oxford and Northampton
Great Britain
Distributed by Password, Manchester

ISBN 0 85646 250 0

A catalogue record for this book
is available from the British Library

Contents

Góngora's Life		9
Góngora Through a Looking-Glass		11
I	A carnation fell	19
II	Climb on my shoulders	23
III	To a Turkish galley's	25
IV	The girl bewailed	29
V	Our native place's	33
VI	Blooms of rosemary	37
VII	Learn to tell, flowers, in me	41
VIII	It is not only nightingales	45
IX	Out of the florid fold	49
X	The Po unbinds crystals	51
XI	Tomorrow, a feast day	53
XII	Easter comes and goes, girls	59
XIII	In a small patch of heaven	63
XIV	Three quatrains	65
XV	To hang from a log, your breast pierced	67
XVI	At your conception free of stain	69
XVII	Sacred temple of sheer modesty	71
XVIII	In night's darkness, on a raging sea	73
XIX	This mount, crowned with crosses	75
XX	Yesterday's human deity, O mortals	77
XXI	To its own element a chaste rose	79
XXII	Funeral machine, yourself unmoving	81
XXIII	Here's a compact key, stranger	83
XXIV	Henry the Fourth lies sorely stabbed	85
XXV	Sacred, towering, gilded pinnacles	87
XXVI	Although not set in metal, the lead's	89
XXVII	Forbidding mountain, vainly set	91
XXVIII	Which of you, fair ladies, would not	93
XXIX	Exalted walls, battlements crowned	95
XXX	O mist of most benignant weather	97
XXXI	Now kissing hands of crystal clearness	99
XXXII	The plume's proud finery had scarcely seen	101
XXXIII	By an ilex tree I used to rest	103

XXXIV	Green rushes of the Duero wove	105
XXXV	Just as at break of day white dew	107
XXXVI	At sunrise while the nymph I love	109
XXXVII	From your divine hand's crystal I drank	111
XXXVIII	To the jointed nacre it was a jail	113
XXXIX	Strange things I've seen, Celalba	115
XL	Astray and sick and wandering	117
XLI	Herein lie entombed the bones of such	119
XLII	If, lovers, you love life, don't touch	121
XLIII	If Love still nesting in its plumes	123
XLIV	Sad sighs of my expressive heart	125
XLV	No wild beast runs, bird flies, fish swims	127
XLVI	Bright glory of the liquid element	129
XLVII	Graceful plants, you who, living	131
XLVIII	At this declining, climacteric	133
XLIX	While burnished gold shines vainly	135
L	A hurtling arrow biting sharp	137
LI	As the short weapon, sharp though healing	139

APPENDICES

1	Góngora's Defence of Poetic Obscurity	143
2	For a black lady's sake	145

NOTES 149
INDEX OF SPANISH FIRST LINES 167

Acknowledgements

WITHOUT THE CONSTANT guidance and unflagging encouragement of my good friend, Luis Huerga, I doubt I would have dared even to approach the work of this great master of the baroque.

Thanks are also due to Don José Paulino of the University of Madrid, to Dr Terry O'Reilly of University College, Cork, and to Peter Jay for his helpful suggestions and his courageous loyalty to a difficult text.

I would also like to acknowledge the stimulation I received from the essays on Góngora by the great Mexican poet, translator and critic, Alfonso Reyes.

And, finally, it should go without saying that Dámaso Alonso's monumental works on Góngora are indispensable reading for anyone who wants to know anything about Góngora.

The Spanish texts accompanying these versions are those of Dámaso Alonso's *Góngora y el 'Polifemo'* (Editorial Gredos, 1967), Biruté Ciplijauskaité's *Luis de Góngora: Sonetos completos* (Clásicos Castalia, 1985) and Antonio Carreño's *Góngora: Romances* (Ediciones Cátedra, 1982).

M.S.

Góngora's Life

THE BASIC FACTS of Góngora's life are as follows. Don Luis de Góngora y Argote, to give the poet his full name, was born in 1561 in the ancient city of Córdoba. His family was comfortably off and well established in the city: his father, Don Francisco de Argote, was a lawyer and a magistrate in Jaén and Madrid; for a time he was also a judge of goods confiscated by the Inquisition. Don Francisco, a highly cultured man with a fine library, encouraged an intellectual life in his home, and he entertained and enjoyed the company of Córdoba's *cognoscenti* such as the humanist Ambrosio de Morales. The poet's mother, Doña Leonor de Góngora, came from a well-connected and affluent family; indeed, her brother, Don Francisco de Góngora, a prebendary of the city's Cathedral, was of considerable importance in Góngora's life, for this uncle decided that he would relinquish some of his ecclesiastical benefices in favour of the poet who, for his part, had to take minor orders to be in benefit while in Salamanca, and later deacon's orders in 1586.

Little is known of Góngora's early years. He was precocious, had a bad accident, and he was involved in a sort of armed fight with some youths of his own class. At fifteen he set off for Salamanca to study law, and during the four years he passed there he managed to over-spend his allowance, was constantly in debt through his gambling at cards (one of his great and lifelong passions), and generally lived the life of the university student away from home. By contrast with the later Góngora, the Góngora of these years seems gaily irresponsible and fun-loving. During this time he began his poetic career, writing his first songs and satires. Before leaving Salamanca he had already acquired a considerable reputation as a poet and wit.

On his return to Córdoba, Góngora had to give serious consideration to his future, and he opted to enter the clerical life in order to inherit legally his uncle's benefices. This did not result, however, in any diminution of the poet's *joie de vivre*. We know this because of a surviving document that records some charges made against Góngora by the new Bishop of Córdoba, Don Francisco Pacheco, in 1588: Góngora is accused of 'rarely participating at choir, of walking about at the set times of prayer, of frequently leaving his seat', and of 'talking a lot during the divine office'. The other charges can be summed up in the fifth charge, that 'he lives like a gallant, and passes his day – and his night – in frivolous things; he keeps the company of theatre people, and he writes profane poetry.'

Góngora defended himself well and with humour against these allegations. It seems that little harm was done to his career by this event, for he was soon undertaking important missions for the Cathedral Chapter (his sonnets record many of these diplomatic journeys, including a long visit in 1603 to the Court at Valladolid). Nevertheless, although he never gave up literary conversation or composition or music (he played the guitar and composed a little), it seems likely that some of his other secular pastimes suffered curtailment.

At this period of his life in his native city Góngora established his reputation as a great poet with the composition of his two major works, the *Fábula de Polifemo y Galatea* and the *Soledades*. His economic situation, however, was not good, and in 1617 he moved to Madrid to take up a royal chaplaincy (for which, of course, he had to be ordained) and to solicit the patronage of such men as Rodrigo Calderón, the Conde de Villamediana and the Conde de Lemos. The poet had high hopes of acquiring fame and wealth for himself and his family.

Góngora spent nine years in Madrid (1617–1626) and his surviving letters of the period are a sad record of his unsuccessful endeavours to obtain the hoped-for patronage, the necessary cost of maintaining himself in good social appearance, his constantly worsening financial situation, his mounting debts, his homesickness, his complaints of family ingratitude and, at the bitter end, his poor health and humiliating indigence. In 1626 Góngora suffered what seems to have been a stroke that left him with no memory of the present but a lucid memory of the past. He died in Córdoba on May 23, 1627.

MICHAEL SMITH

Góngora Through a Looking-Glass

ALTHOUGH MANY of Góngora's poems begin with a detail or incident from what is usually referred to as 'common reality' (a lady cuts her finger as she removes a ring; the form and colour of flowers; Góngora notes a mountain in Granada on which in the past Christian anchorites lived and were buried; a royal catafalque is observed; a king dies), these initiatory details or incidents are densely elaborated until they become barely perceptible in the overall effect of the poem. While there is usually something to be gained by the reader referring back to these details or to the 'common reality' from which they are derived, the fact is that the poems are made, not out of 'common reality', however mediated, but out of literature, which is thoroughly mediated. This gives Góngora's poems the effect of occurring at a very great remove from 'reality', and thus, as though through a series of inter-reflecting mirrors, of having only the most tenuous relationship with the 'ordinary world'.

In consequence, the reading of Góngora requires a certain adjustment of one's normal reading habits. The poems are neither functional (informational or propagandist) nor simply escapist; rather, they are ornamental – in the best sense of the word, that is to say, intrinsically – and they yield intelligibility only to an aesthetic approach. As with a jewel, the relevant question to ask is not what it does, but how its beauty has been achieved. Of course, just as with a jewel, one may inquire what sociological purpose it serves; for instance, to reinforce the élitism of a ruling-class. But that is another matter: literature in the class-struggle.

The great Mexican critic Alfonso Reyes writes that Góngora, aside from the fact that a whole beat of historical consciousness separates him from us, is not a poet of the spirit but a poet of the senses. In him we meet secrets and technical delights of form, never sentimental tremblings or lofty situations. We should study him, Reyes advises, as an object of exclusive and pure aesthetic contemplation.

Góngora's *culteranismo* may well be understood in this aesthetic context. Its allusions to classical mythology are not to lend weight and dignity to Góngora's own poetry; rather,

Góngora's imagination is thoroughly imbued with the classical mythological world, and that world of mythology, interposed between Góngora and 'reality', is involved in a process of mediation through which common-sense reality is transformed and endowed with aesthetic standing. It is a process of Ovidian metamorphosis, the ordinary being imaginatively and magically transformed into the fabulous which alone satisfies Góngora's aesthetic sensibility.

This obviously baroque Góngora, however, is not the only Góngora. There is also the early Góngora of the *romances* or ballads; and while Góngora's ballads are never simple, as Dámaso Alonso has repeatedly cautioned, by contrast with the fabulously ornate art of the *Soledades* or the *Polifemo*, they possess a candidness, a directness, that strikes the reader familiar with the *Soledades* as paradoxical. I suggest that the key to this paradox is to be found in the *form* of the poems. Whereas in the *arte mayor* of the *Soledades*, Góngora achieves a distancing of reality by means of the very material he is using, in the *romances* the self-conscious instrumentality of the popular form permits him a similar degree of distancing. He can use the *persona* of the anonymous balladeer without fear of ascription to himself of what he may say or observe.

Essentially, Góngora is a verbal magician, a transmuter of reality, both observed and literary. It goes without saying that a good deal of creative literature can be viewed as transmutation or mediation, to use a more current term. Yet the unfailing persistence of Góngora in elaborating the given, and the degree of that elaboration, is remarkable and characteristic, and points to something central to the poet.

To look to Góngora's poems for intimately personal revelation is inevitably to be disappointed. Góngora's intention as a poet was far removed from such indulgence. Mallarmé could have been writing of Góngora's poetry when he wrote: 'The pure work implies the elocutory disappearance of the poet who abandons the initiative to words mobilized by the shock of their inequality; they light on one another with mutual reflections like a virtual trail of fire upon precious stones, replacing the breathing perceptible in the old lyrical blast or the enthusiastic personal direction of the phrase.' 'To speak,' Mallarmé wrote, 'has no connexion with the reality of things except commercially: in literature it is content to make an allusion to them or to separate their quality which will be embodied in some idea.' (Mallarmé's 'Variations sur un sujet' in Anthony Hartley's Penguin edition, 1965).

A striking illustration of Góngora's poetic sensibility, the procedure of his poetic composition, may be obtained by comparing the sonnet 'Ya besando unas manos cristalinas' with Ovid's *Amores* I.5 (which I think can be taken as having been read by Góngora). Ovid's poem, as one would expect, is erotically explicit. In Marlowe's translation:

> Then came Corinna in a long loose gown,
> Her white neck hid with tresses hanging down . . .
> Stark naked as she stood before mine eye,
> Not one wen in her body could I spy.
> What arms and shoulders did I touch and see,
> How apt her breasts were to be pressed by me!
> How smooth a belly under her waist saw I,
> How large a leg, and what a lusty thigh!

By contrast, Góngora's poem de-eroticizes both the lady's beauty and the love-making. Her hands are 'of crystal clearness'; her hair is 'gold'; her teeth 'fine pearls'; her lips 'scarlet roses'; Góngora may clasp the lady's 'white smooth neck' but he does not deign to press her breasts. The essential difference between the two poems is that while the arousal of the erotic impulse is the aim of the Ovid poem – the poem has a non-literary end, so to speak – for Góngora the lady's beauty and the barely suggested love-making are merely so much material (licensed by convention) to be used in the creation of the poem. The potential eroticism of the material is subdued for the sake of what Góngora considers the higher good of aesthetic excellence.

In his famous essay on Góngora, 'The Poetic Image in Don Luis de Góngora', Lorca insists, persuasively, that Góngora cultivated the image as the essence of poetry. It is not necessary to agree fully with Lorca to see how important the image is to Góngora: indisputably, it is a powerful means of distancing and subordinating the contingent reality from which it is derived. On the relationship between Góngora's images and that objective world, Lorca writes with a poet's perception:

Of course, Góngora does not fashion his images on Nature itself but rather brings the object, thing or action into the darkroom of his brain and from there it emerges transformed to leap on that other world with which it is fused. Therefore his poetry, as it is not direct, cannot be read in face of the objects to which it refers. The poplars, roses, shepherdesses and seas of his spiritual Córdoba are newly created. He calls the sea 'a rough diamond, set in marble, ever undulant', or the poplar 'a green lyre.' Nothing can be more misguided than to read his madrigal to a rose with a rose in one's hand. Either the rose or the madrigal should be sufficient.

It seems to me that Góngora's essential difference from other baroque poets is not to be found either in the material of his conceits or even in their variety. Donne, Cowley, Cleveland, Crashaw, not to mention Quevedo, deploy conceits as variously and as ingeniously as Góngora. But whereas for these, even for the wildly extravagant Cleveland, the conceit is ultimately justifiable by reference to a moral or immoral lesson, for Góngora the real interest is in the conceit itself: Góngora's difference is his preparedness to be absorbed in the conceit, to accept it, not merely analogously but as substantial in its own right, as a legitimate object of our attention and aesthetic pleasure. It is precisely to his delight in the conceit itself that Roy Campbell refers when he describes how Góngora's 'far-fetched images and metaphors collide and splinter kaleidoscopically into the most dazzling patterns' (in Campbell's *Lorca: An Appreciation of His Poetry*, Bowes & Bowes, 1952).

There is an extremeness about Góngora's conceits that is not mere fancifulness, but the result of the pressure of a problematic contingent reality. Let us take, as illustration, the sonnet 'Oh claro honor del líquido elemento'. In this poem the lady whose image is reflected on the water's surface is not the subject of the poem. Rather, it is the conceit of the reflected image on the level surface of the smooth-flowing stream not being shattered by a sudden turbulence in the stream's current, so that the image of beauty can pass on intact in its loveliness to Neptune, god of the sea. Of course, the conceit can be interpreted as a comment on the precarious fragility of human beauty and indeed on the futility of the poet's passion for that beauty; but the poem's real delight lies in the aesthetic pleasure of the conceit itself.

And therein lies the modernity of Góngora: his conviction and demonstration of the substantial reality of the literary artifact. Góngora achieves in his poems the liberation of language from its traditional bondage to a correspondent reality. The French Symbolists had a precursor in Góngora; and it does not seem to me coincidental that the great rediscovery of Góngora in Spain occurred at a time when Spanish poetry was under the influence of French poetic modernism. Just as in the twentieth century, painters, released from the necessity of the representational function, were free to explore the aesthetic possibilities of colour and form as things in their own right, Góngora, centuries before, had discovered and exploited a similar freedom in literature. No wonder Roy Campbell wrote of him that 'he is a symbolist who contains the whole of Mallarmé and a lot more besides, a symbolist three hundred years before his time.'

The old critical bugbear of Góngora's obscurity may perhaps be seen now in a new light. Góngora, on his own admission, was deliberately élitist in his poetic composition.* Like Mallarmé, his intention was to create a poetry that would be as 'undefiled' by temporality as that of his beloved classical Latin masters. His method of doing that was to attempt to strip it of practical contingency, of local colour and topic; to use the Spanish language with what seemed to him the timelessness of Vergil's Latin. The alleged obscurity of Góngora's poetry is a deliberately contrived barrier to exclude the *ignorantes* for whom the only reality is that of practical common-sense. Góngora made no apologies for this.

Finally the inevitable question of Góngora and Quevedo, *culteranismo* and *conceptismo*, the old polarities, the old enmities. Despite his passionate and often malicious rivalry, Quevedo could not, any more than others, escape the influence of Góngora. Although both were masters of the craft of verse, the difference between them is crucial.

For all his passion, of love and hate, Quevedo was primarily a reasoner, a man of acutely critical intelligence. In him the

---

* See Appendix 1.

mind is always dominant, defining and pointing feelings. Góngora, no less intelligent, is, however, more expansive intellectually. His personality, his temperament, is more relaxed, more self-assured; his aesthetic sensibility more prevalent and decisive in giving shape to his poems. What matters for Góngora is the weight and texture of the words he uses, the resonance of the imagery recalling the classical past, Vergil and Ovid, resonating with subtle echoes. His inversions are not due to the contingencies of rhyme and metre, but a means of placing a word so that it can be savoured for all its rich qualities. Quevedo, on the other hand, is never relaxed. He is always irritated, perturbed, cutting and thrusting, mimetic of the man of action. Góngora, perhaps more wise, if less prominent in the ways of the world than Quevedo, is patient, his lethal wit less frenetic but equally efficient. His voice, for all its verbal luxuriance, sounds a note of restrained melancholy. A sense of mortality adds poignancy to his evocations of the beautiful, even in the candid freshness of his *romances* or ballads.

MICHAEL SMITH

Luis de Góngora

Selected Shorter Poems

I

*Caído se le ha un clavel
hoy a la Aurora del seno:
¡qué glorioso que está el heno,
porque ha caído sobre él!*

Cuando el silencio tenía
todas las cosas del suelo,
y coronada del yelo
reinaba la noche fría,
en medio la monarquía
de tiniebla tan crüel,
    *caído se le ha un clavel
    hoy a la Aurora del seno:
    ¡qué glorioso que está el heno,
    porque ha caído sobre él!*

De un solo clavel ceñida
la Virgen, aurora bella,
al mundo se le dio, y ella
quedó cual antes florida;
a la púrpura caída
sólo fue el heno fiel.
    *Caído se le ha un clavel
    hoy a la Aurora del seno:
    ¡qué glorioso que está el heno,
    porque ha caído sobre él!*

El heno, pues, que fue dino,
a pesar de tantas nieves,
de ver en sus brazos leves
este rosicler divino,

I

*A carnation fell
from the bosom of dawn:
how glorious the hay
that it fell upon!*

While silence held sway
over things of the earth,
and the cold night reigned
in its diadem of ice,
in the midst of the kingdom
of such cruel dark,
> *a carnation fell
> from the bosom of dawn:
> how glorious the hay
> that it fell upon!*

The Virgin, fair dawn,
with a single pink girt,
gave it to the world
while staying in bloom;
to the crimson that fell
only hay proved true.
> *A carnation fell
> from the bosom of dawn:
> how glorious the hay
> that it fell upon!*

Proved of its trueness
despite many snows,
to see in its light arms
this heavenly glow,

para su lecho fue lino,
oro para su dosel.
> *Caído se le ha un clavel*
> *hoy a la Aurora del seno:*
> *¡qué glorioso que está el heno,*
> *porque ha caído sobre él!*

for its cot hay was linen,
for its canopy, gold.
> *A carnation fell*
> *from the bosom of dawn:*
> *how glorious the hay*
> *that it fell upon!*

II

Oveja perdida, ven
sobre mis hombros, que hoy
no sólo tu pastor soy,
sino tu pasto también.

Por descubrirte mejor
cuando balabas perdida,
dejé en un árbol la vida,
donde me subió el amor;
si prenda quieres mayor,
mis obras hoy te la den.
> *Oveja perdida, ven*
> *sobre mis hombros, que hoy*
> *no sólo tu pastor soy,*
> *sino tu pasto también.*

Pasto al fin hoy tuyo hecho,
¿cuál dará mayor asombro,
o el traerte yo en el hombro,
o el traerme tú en el pecho?
Prendas son de amor estrecho
que aun los más ciegos las ven.
> *Oveja perdida, ven*
> *sobre mis hombros, que hoy*
> *no sólo tu pastor soy,*
> *sino tu pasto también.*

II

Climb on my shoulders,
sheep who are lost,
today I am not only
pastor but pasture.

The better to find you,
bleating and astray,
I left my love upon a tree
where love had lifted me.
If greater pledge you need
my deeds give it this day.
> *Climb on my shoulders,*
> *sheep who are lost,*
> *today I am not only*
> *pastor but pasture.*

Made food for you this day,
which more surprises you:
that I bear you on my shoulders?
Or you bear me in your breast?
Both are pledges of love
even the blindest see.
> *Climb on my shoulders,*
> *sheep who are lost,*
> *today I am not only*
> *pastor but pasture.*

III

Amarrado al duro banco
de una galera turquesca,
ambas manos en el remo
y ambos ojos en la tierra,

un forzado de Dragut
en la playa de Marbella
se quejaba al ronco son
del remo y de la cadena:

«¡Oh sagrado mar de España,
famosa playa serena,
teatro donde se han hecho
cien mil navales tragedias!,

pues eres tú el mismo mar
que con tus crecientes besas
las murallas de mi patria,
coronadas y soberbias,

tráeme nuevas de mi esposa,
y dime si han sido ciertas
las lágrimas y suspiros
que me dice por sus letras;

porque si es verdad que llora
mi cautiverio en tu arena,
bien puedes al mar del Sur
vencer en lucientes perlas.

III

To a Turkish galley's
hard bench bound,
both hands on the oar,
on the land both eyes,

an oarsman of Dragut
in Marbella bay
moaned to the rasp
of oar and chain:

'O Spain's sacred sea,
shore famed and serene,
where ten thousand tragedies
of the sea have been staged!

Since you are the sea
that kiss with your tides
my homeland's walls
turreted and proud,

bring me news from my spouse
and say if true
are the tears and the sighs
her letters report;

if indeed my bondage
she wails on your sands,
you're sure to surpass
the South Sea in pearls.

Dame ya, sagrado mar,
a mis demandas respuesta,
que bien puedes, si es verdad
que las aguas tienen lengua;

pero, pues no me respondes,
sin duda alguna que es muerta,
aunque no lo debe ser
pues que vivo yo en su ausencia.

Pues he vivido diez años
sin libertad y sin ella,
siempre al remo condenado,
a nadie matarán penas.»

En esto se descubrieron
de la Religión seis velas,
y el cómitre mandó usar
al forzado de su fuerza.

Sacred sea, answer soon
the questions I put,
for you can, if it's true
that the water has tongues.

But since you won't answer,
she must now be dead;
though how can she die
and I still live on?

Condemned to the oar
ten years I have lived
unfree and without her,
death's lost all its ill.'

Six sails of the Order
were seen then on course.
And the oarsmate ordered
the forced one to force.

IV

Lloraba la niña
(y tenía razón)
la prolija ausencia
de su ingrato amor.

Dejóla tan niña,
que apenas, creo yo,
que tenía los años
que ha que la dejó.

Llorando la ausencia
del galán traidor,
la halla la luna
y la deja el sol,

añadiendo siempre
pasión a pasión,
memoria a memoria,
dolor a dolor.

> *Llorad, corazón,*
> *que tenéis razón.*

Dícele su madre:
«Hija, por mi amor,
que se acabe el llanto,
o me acabe yo.»

Ella le responde:
«No podrá ser, no;
las causas son muchas,
los ojos son dos.

IV

The girl bewailed
(and with good cause)
the long absence
of her ingrate love.

He took his leave
when she was young,
I think no older
than the years he's gone.

Her the sun left
the moon discovers,
grieving the loss
of a faithless lover.

Forever adding
passion to passion,
memory to memory,
sorrow to sorrow.

> *Mourn, my heart,*
> *for you've good cause.*

The mother urges:
'Daughter, for love,
put an end to weeping
or my life's done.'

'No, I cannot,'
she makes reply,
'The causes are many,
but two these eyes.

Satisfagan, madre,
tanta sinrazón
y lágrimas lloren
en esta ocasión,

tantas como de ellos
un tiempo tiró
flechas amorosas
el arquero dios.

Ya no canto, madre,
y si canto yo,
muy tristes endechas
mis canciones son;

porque el que se fue,
con lo que llevó,
se dejó el silencio,
y llevó la voz.»

*Llorad, corazón,
que tenéis razón.*

May they, Mother,
now atone,
for so much folly
and let tears flow

from them in plenty
as from them once
were sent love's arrows
by the archer god.

I give up song, Mother,
but if I should sing,
let my songs be dirges
of very sad ring.

For he who departed
took with him along
what left only silence
and carried off song.'

> *Mourn, my heart,*
> *for you've good cause.*

V

La más bella niña
de nuestro lugar,
hoy vïuda y sola
y ayer por casar,
viendo que sus ojos
a la guerra van,
a su madre dice,
que escucha su mal:
    dejadme llorar
    orillas del mar.

Pues me distes, madre,
en tan tierna edad
tan corto el placer,
tan largo el pesar,
y me cautivastes
de quien hoy se va
y lleva las llaves
de mi libertad:
    dejadme llorar
    orillas del mar.

En llorar conviertan
mis ojos, de hoy más,
el sabroso oficio
del dulce mirar,
pues que no se pueden
mejor ocupar,
yéndose a la guerra
quien era mi paz:
    dejadme llorar
    orillas del mar.

V

Our native place's
loveliest lass,
today a lone widow,
yesterday not matched,
on seeing her darling
for the wars depart,
complains to her mother
who listens to her harms.
>   *Leave me weep*
>   *by the ocean deep.*

Since you gave me, Mother,
at such tender age,
so short-lived a pleasure,
so lasting a pain,
and you made me captive
to him who flees today
and the keys of my freedom
takes with him away,
>   *leave me weep*
>   *by the ocean deep.*

From the savoury labour
of gentle sight,
henceforth to weeping
turn then my eyes;
now for better uses
they've lost their might
since the man of my peace
fell to war's plight.
>   *Leave me weep*
>   *by the ocean deep.*

No me pongáis freno
ni queráis culpar;
que lo uno es justo,
lo otro por demás.
Si me queréis bien
no me hagáis mal;
harto peor fuera
morir y callar:
>   *dejadme llorar*
>   *orillas del mar.*

Dulce madre mía,
¿quién no llorará
aunque tenga el pecho
como un pedernal,
y no dará voces
viendo marchitar
los más verdes años
de mi mocedad?
>   *Dejadme llorar*
>   *orillas del mar.*

Váyanse las noches,
pues ido se han
los ojos que hacían
los míos velar;
váyanse y no vean
tanta soledad,
después que en mi lecho
sobra la mitad:
>   *dejadme llorar*
>   *orillas del mar.*

Put no check upon me
nor load me with guilt;
for the one is justice,
the other of no avail;
would you show me favour?
Then do me no ill.
Far worse would I fare
if dead and laid still.
> *Leave me weep*
> *by the ocean deep.*

Would not, sweet Mother,
even he lament
who'd boast a breast
as hard as flint,
and would he not clamour
while he beheld
youth's greenest years
wither to death?
> *Leave me weep*
> *by the ocean deep.*

Let the nights depart,
for those eyes have gone
that made mine attend
as the nights came on;
let them go, not seeing
my solitude's bond –
by a half too large
this couch I lie on.
> *Leave me weep*
> *by the ocean deep.*

VI

Las flores del romero,
niña Isabel,
hoy son flores azules,
mañana serán miel.

Celosa estás, la niña,
celosa estás de aquel
dichoso, pues le buscas,
ciego, pues no te ve,
ingrato, pues te enoja,
y confiado, pues
no se disculpa hoy
de lo que hizo ayer.
Enjuguen esperanzas
lo que lloras por él;
que celos entre aquellos
que se han querido bien,
> *hoy son flores azules,*
> *mañana serán miel.*

Aurora de ti misma,
que cuando a amanecer
a tu placer empiezas,
te eclipsan tu placer,
serénense tus ojos,
y más perlas no des,
porque al Sol le está mal
lo que a la Aurora bien.
Desata, como nieblas,
todo lo que ves;

VI

Blooms of rosemary,
Isabel, love,
today are blue flowers,
but honey anon.

Jealous, dear, jealous
are you of him there,
blest that you seek him,
though he's blind to your care;
thankless, he angers,
self-assured his poise,
today not disclaiming
yesterday's wrong.
Let hope wipe out
all you weep for him,
for jealousies
of those who've loved
  today are blue flowers,
  but honey anon.

Dawn of yourself,
for whom pleasure's eclipsed
as you to pleasure
were about to wake;
let your eyes be still,
yield no more pearls,
for what befits daybreak
ill becomes the sun.
Dispel as if mists
all you can't view;

que sospechas de amantes
y querellas después,
    hoy son flores azules,
    mañana serán miel.

for lovers' suspicions
and rows that ensue
> *today are blue flowers*
> *but honey anon.*

VII

Aprended, flores, en mí
lo que va de ayer a hoy,
que ayer maravilla fui,
y sombra mía aun no soy.

La Aurora ayer me dio cuna,
la noche ataúd me dio:
sin luz muriera, si no
me la prestara la Luna.
Pues de vosotras ninguna
deja de acabar así,
    aprended, flores, en mí
    lo que va de ayer a hoy,
    que ayer maravilla fui,
    y sombra mía aun no soy.

Consuelo dulce el clavel
es a la breve edad mía,
pues quien me concedió un día,
dos apenas le dio a él;
efímeras del vergel,
yo cárdena, él carmesí,
    aprended, flores, en mí
    lo que va de ayer a hoy,
    que ayer maravilla fui,
    y sombra mía aun no soy.

Flor es el jazmín, si bella,
no de las más vividoras,
pues dura pocas más horas
que rayos tiene de estrella;

VII

Learn to tell, flowers, in me,
the lapse from eve to morrow;
marvellous marigold of yesterday,
I'm now not my own shadow.

Dawn yesterday gave me a cot,
night gave to me a coffin;
without light I would have died
but for what the moon sent me.
Since none of you shall fail to die
in the way that I describe,
>   *learn to tell, flowers, in me,*
>   *the lapse from eve to morrow;*
>   *marvellous marigold of yesterday,*
>   *I'm now not my own shadow.*

The sweet carnation is a balm
to my own life's brief stretch of time:
he who granted me one day
awarded to it scarcely two;
mayflies of the garden, I'm
the purple, it the crimson bloom.
>   *Learn to tell, flowers, in me,*
>   *the lapse from eve to morrow;*
>   *marvellous marigold of yesterday,*
>   *I'm now not my own shadow.*

Though beautiful, the jasmine's not
among the longest living flowers;
it scarcely lives a few more hours
than the starlight rays it hosts;

si el ámbar florece, es ella
la flor que él retiene en sí.
> *Aprended, flores, en mí*
> *lo que va de ayer a hoy,*
> *que ayer maravilla fui,*
> *y sombra mía aun no soy.*

Aunque el alhelí grosero
en fragancia y en color,
más días ve que otra flor,
pues ve los de un mayo entero,
morir maravilla quiero,
y no vivir alhelí.
> *Aprended, flores, en mí*
> *lo que va de ayer a hoy,*
> *que ayer maravilla fui,*
> *y sombra mía aun no soy.*

A ninguna al fin mayores
términos concede el sol
si no es al girasol,
Matusalén de las flores;
ojos son aduladores
cuantas en él hojas vi.
> *Aprended, flores, en mí*
> *lo que va de ayer a hoy,*
> *que ayer maravilla fui,*
> *y sombra mía aun no soy.*

if amber can be said to bloom,
this flower all amber boasts.
>   *Learn to tell, flowers, in me,*
>   *the lapse from eve to morrow;*
>   *marvellous marigold of yesterday,*
>   *I'm now not my own shadow.*

Although in scent and colour coarse,
the gillyflower beholds more days
than any other flower in bloom,
for it beholds the whole of May;
yet I'll not live as gillyflower,
but pass away as marigold.
>   *Learn to tell, flowers, in me,*
>   *the lapse from eve to morrow;*
>   *marvellous marigold of yesterday,*
>   *I'm now not my own shadow.*

That Methuselah of flowers,
the sunflower, only being exempt,
the sun at length concedes
terms no longer to any bloom;
where all the leaves I saw
are as many coaxing eyes.
>   *Learn to tell, flowers, in me,*
>   *the lapse from eve to morrow;*
>   *marvellous marigold of yesterday,*
>   *I'm now not my own shadow.*

VIII

No son todos ruiseñores
los que cantan entre las flores,
sino campanitas de plata,
que tocan a la alba;
sino trompeticas de oro,
que hacen la salva
a los soles que adoro.

No todas las voces ledas
son de sirenas con plumas
cuyas húmidas espumas
son las verdes alamedas.
Si suspendido te quedas
a los süaves clamores,
  no son todos ruiseñores
  los que cantan entre las flores,
  sino campanitas de plata,
  que tocan a la alba;
  sino trompeticas de oro,
  que hacen la salva
  a los soles que adoro.

Lo artificioso que admira,
y lo dulce que consuela,
no es de aquel violín que vuela
ni de esotra inquieta lira;
otro instrumento es quien tira
de los sentidos mejores:
  no son todos ruiseñores
  los que cantan entre las flores,
  sino campanitas de plata,
  que tocan a la alba;

VIII

It is not only nightingales
that sing among the flowers,
but little silver bells
that chime at dawning hour;
but tiny golden trumpets
that play a serenade
to the suns I adore.

Not all the lovely voices
belong to plumaged sirens
whose splashing sprays are
the green poplar groves.
Should you remain enthralled
by their gentle sounds,
> *it is not only nightingales*
> *that sing among the flowers,*
> *but little silver bells*
> *that chime at dawning hour;*
> *but tiny golden trumpets*
> *that play a serenade*
> *to the suns I adore.*

Astounding artifice,
sweetness that assuages,
are not that flying fiddle's
nor of that lyre's rages;
it's another instrument
plucks the keenest senses:
> *it is not only nightingales*
> *that sing among the flowers,*
> *but little silver bells*
> *that chime at dawning hour;*

sino trompeticas de oro,
que hacen la salva
a los soles que adoro.

Las campanitas luzientes,
y los dorados clarines
en coronados jazmines,
los dos hermosos corrientes
no sólo recuerdan gentes
sino convocan amores.
No son todos ruiseñores
los que cantan entre las flores,
sino campanitas de plata,
que tocan a la alba;
sino trompeticas de oro,
que hacen la salva
a los soles que adoro.

> *but tiny golden trumpets*
> *that play a serenade*
> *to the suns I adore.*

The tiny shining bells
and the gilded bugles
in the crowned jasmines,
the two lovely streams
not only waken people
but summon them to love.
> *It is not only nightingales*
> *that sing among the flowers,*
> *but little silver bells*
> *that chime at dawning hour;*
> *but tiny golden trumpets*
> *that play a serenade*
> *to the suns I adore.*

IX

De la florida falda
que hoy de perlas bordó la alba luciente,
tejidos en guirnalda
traslado estos jazmines a tu frente,
que piden, con ser flores,
blanco a tus sienes y a tu boca olores.

Guarda destos jazmines,
de abejas era un escuadrón volante,
ronco, sí, de clarines,
mas de puntas armado de diamante;
púselas en huída,
y cada flor me cuesta una herida.

Más, Clori, que he tejido
jazmines al cabello desatado,
y más besos te pido
que abejas tuvo el escuadrón armado;
lisonjas son iguales
servir yo en flores, pagar tú en panales.

IX

Out of the florid fold
bright dawn fretted in pearls today,
into a garland woven
these jasmines on your head I lay;
although flowers, they seek
your forehead's white and your mouth's scent.

A flying squad of honeybees,
these jasmines' sentry-guard;
their voice husky of clarions
though with points of diamond armed;
I forced them all to flee,
and each flower meant a wound to me.

More kisses I beg of you
than jasmines I wove in your strewn hair,
and more than the bees, Clori,
that in the armoured squadrons were;
our love's reciprocation is
I court in flowers, you pay in honeycombs.

X

Cristales el Po desata,
que al hijo fueron del Sol,
si trémulo no farol,
túmulo de undosa plata;
las espumosas dilata
armas de sañudo toro,
contra arquitecto canoro,
que orilla el Tajo eterniza
la fulminada ceniza
en simétrica urna de oro.

X

The Po unbinds crystals;
to the sun's child they were
if not a wavering torch,
a vault of waving silver;
it shows – a fearsome bull –
its frothy arms-of-war
against the melodious
architect who, ashore
the Tagus, immortalizes
the fulminated ash
in symmetric urn of gold.

XI

Hermana Marica,
mañana, que es fiesta,
no irás tú a la amiga
ni yo iré a la escuela.

Pondráste el corpiño
y la saya buena,
cabezón labrado,
toca y albanega;

y a mí me pondrán
mi camisa nueva,
sayo de palmilla,
media de estameña;

y si hace bueno
trairé la montera
que me dio la Pascua
mi señora abuela,

y el estadal rojo
con lo que le cuelga,
que trajo el vecino
cuando fue a la feria.

Iremos a misa,
veremos la iglesia,
darános un cuarto
mi tía la ollera.

XI

Tomorrow, a feast day,
Marica, sister,
I'll forsake the school,
you the schoolmistress.

You'll dress up in bodice
and in your fine frock,
with colour embroidered,
hair-net and coif;

they'll get me up
in a new shirt,
a woollen suit
and socks of serge;

and the weather fine,
I'll wear the cap
my Grandma sent
this Easter last,

and the red neck-ribbon
with tassels hung,
a prize from the fair
the neighbour brought.

We'll go to Mass,
we'll view the church;
my potter-aunt
won't see us short.

Compraremos de él
(que nadie lo sepa)
chochos y garbanzos
para la merienda;

y en la tardecica,
en nuestra plazuela,
jugaré yo al toro
y tú a las muñecas

con las dos hermanas
Juana y Madalena
y las dos primillas
María y la tuerta;

y si quiere madre
dar las castañetas,
podrás tanto de ello
bailar en la puerta;

y al son del adufe
cantará Andrehuela:
«no me aprovecharon,
madre, las hierbas»;

y yo de papel
haré una librea
teñida con moras
porque bien parezca,

y una caperuza
con muchas almenas;
pondré por penacho
las dos plumas negras

And we shall buy
(behind their backs)
chickpeas, dainties
for our snack.

And in our small square
when evening falls
I'll play bull-fighter
and you'll play dolls

With the two sisters,
Juana, Madalena,
and the two little cousins,
María and the squinty one.

And if Mother will give
the castanets, you can dance
as much as you like
at the door of the house;

Andrehuela will sing
to the timbrel's sound:
'Mother, the herbs . . .
they did me no good.'

And I'll make from paper
a livery,
in mulberry dyed
so it looks fine,

and I'll make a hood
that's castellated;
and for its plume
use two black feathers

del rabo del gallo,
que acullá en la huerta
anaranjeamos
las Carnestolendas;

y en la caña larga
pondré una bandera
con dos borlas blancas
en sus tranzaderas;

y en mi caballito
pondré una cabeza
de guadamecí,
dos hilos por riendas;

y entraré en la calle
haciendo corvetas
yo, y otros del barrio,
que son más de treinta.

Jugaremos cañas
junto a la plazuela
porque Barbolilla
salga acá y nos vea;

Barbola, la hija
de la panadera,
la que suele darme
tortas con manteca,

porque algunas veces
hacemos yo y ella
las bellaquerías
detrás de la puerta.

from that cock's tail
we'd pelt with oranges
there at Shrovetide
in the orchard;

and on the long pole
I'll hang a flag
with two white tufts
made in its cords;

and I shall furnish
with a leathern head
my small toy horse,
his reins two threads;

then out on the street
with a leap and a bound,
my friends and I
making a crowd.

We'll play at jousting
in the little square
so Barbolilla
pops out and stares;

that Barbola,
the baker's daughter,
who often gives me
griddle cakes;

for sometimes she
and I conspire
to play some tricks
behind the door.

XII

¡Que se nos va la Pascua, mozas,
que se nos va la Pascua!

Mozuelas las de mi barrio,
loquillas y confiadas,
mirad no os engañe el tiempo,
la edad y la confianza.
No os dejéis lisonjear
de la juventud lozana,
porque de caducas flores
teje el tiempo sus guirnaldas.
¡Que se nos va la Pascua, mozas,
que se nos va la Pascua!

Vuelan los ligeros años,
y con presurosas alas
nos roban, como harpías,
nuestras sabrosas viandas.
La flor de la maravilla
esta verdad nos declara,
porque le hurta la tarde
lo que le dio la mañana.
¡Que se nos va la Pascua, mozas,
que se nos va la Pascua!

Mirad que cuando pensáis
que hacen la señal de la alba
las campanas de la vida,
es la queda, y os desarma
de vuestro color y lustre,
de vuestro donaire y gracia,

XII

Easter comes and goes, girls,
   Easter comes and goes.

Girls of my place,
wild and assured,
don't let time cheat,
nor age and trust fool.
Do not be flattered
by youth's lush hours:
time weaves its garlands
with short-lived flowers.
   Easter comes and goes, girls,
      Easter comes and goes.

The quick years fly,
and on speeding wings
they rob us like harpies
of our savoury things.
The marigold's bloom
this truth reveals,
for what morning gave
the evening steals.
   Easter comes and goes, girls,
      Easter comes and goes.

When life's bells ring
what you think is dawn,
it's curfew you hear
and you are stripped bare
of charm and of grace,
of colour and gloss,

y quedáis todas perdidas
por mayores de la marca.
 ¡Que se nos va la Pascua, mozas,
 que se nos va la Pascua!

Yo sé de una buena vieja
que fue un tiempo rubia y zarca,
y que al presente le cuesta
harto caro el ver su cara:
porque su bruñida frente
y sus mejillas se hallan
más que roquete de obispo
encogidas y arrugadas.
 ¡Que se nos va la Pascua, mozas,
 que se nos va la Pascua!

Y sé de otra buena vieja
que un diente que le quedaba
se lo dejó estotro día
sepultado en unas natas:
y con lágrimas le dice:
«Diente mío de mi alma,
yo sé cuando fuistes perla,
aunque ahora no sois nada».
 ¡Que se nos va la Pascua, mozas,
 que se nos va la Pascua!

Por eso, mozuelas locas,
antes que la edad avara
el rubio cabello de oro
convierta en luciente plata,
quered cuando sois queridas,
amad cuando sois amadas:
mirad, bobas, que detrás
se pinta la ocasión calva.
 ¡Que se nos va la Pascua, mozas,
 que se nos va la Pascua!

and you who stay in,
outlast and are lost.
> *Easter comes and goes, girls,*
> > *Easter comes and goes.*

I know an old dear
who was blue-eyed and fair
now counts it no trifle
to see her own face;
for a bishop's surplice
is less shrunk and creased
than those cheeks and brow
of hers, burnished once.
> *Easter comes and goes, girls,*
> > *Easter comes and goes.*

And another I know
whose one last molar
dropped out at last
and sank in some custard.
'O dear tooth of mine,'
to tears she is wrought,
'I once knew you a pearl,
and now you are naught.'
> *Easter comes and goes, girls,*
> > *Easter comes and goes.*

And so, reckless girls,
before greedy age
turns to bright silver
your fair golden hair,
court when you're courted,
love when you're loved;
take heed, silly girls,
Fate's nape is bald.
> *Easter comes and goes, girls,*
> > *Easter comes and goes.*

XIII

En dos lucientes estrellas,
y estrellas de rayos negros,
dividido he visto el Sol
en breve espacio de cielo.

El luciente oficio hacen
de las estrellas de Venus
las mañanas como el Alba,
las noches como el Lucero.

Las formas perfilan de oro,
milagosamente haciendo,
no las bellezas oscuras,
sino los oscuros bellos,

y cuyos rayos para él
son las llaves de su puerto,
si tiene puertos un mar
que es todo golfos y estrechos.

Pero no son tan piadosos,
aunque sí lo son, pues vemos
que visten rayos de luto
por cuantas vidas han muerto.

XIII

In a small patch of heaven
I saw the sun unseam,
become two shining stars
and these had black beams.

They shine and serve
as the Venus stars:
at dawn the morning star,
the evening star at night.

Their shapes rimmed in gold,
a miracle is worked:
the dark becomes fair,
not the fair dark.

Rays that are the keys
to this sea's port
if ports become a sea
all gulfs and straits.

Eyes with no such mercy –
but yet they have, look!
The rays they don in mourning
for so many lives wrecked.

XIV

Tres seguidillas

i

Mátanme los celos
de aquel andaluz,
háganme si muriere
la mortaja azul.

ii

Perdí la esperanza
de ver mi ausente:
háganme si muriere
la mortaja verde.

iii

La mitad del alma
me lleva la mar:
volved, galeritas,
por la otra mitad.

XIV

Three quatrains

i

I'm killed with pangs
for that Andaluz;
if I should die
clothe me in blue.

ii

Hopeless of seeing
my absent love,
if I should die
clothe me in green.

iii

Half of my soul
the sea bears off:
dear galleys, return
for the other half.

XV

Pender de un leño, traspasado el pecho,
y de espinas clavadas ambas sienes,
dar tus mortales penas en rehenes
de nuestra gloria, bien fue heroico hecho;

pero más fue nacer en tanto estrecho,
donde, para mostrar en nuestros bienes
a dónde bajas y de dónde vienes,
no quiere un portalillo tener techo.

No fue ésta más hazaña, oh gran Dios mío,
del tiempo, por haber la helada ofensa
vencido en flaca edad con pecho fuerte

(que más fue sudar sangre que haber frío),
sino porque hay distancia más inmensa
de Dios a hombre, que de hombre a muerte.

XV

To hang from a log, your breast pierced,
both temples nailed with thorns, to give
your deadly griefs as hostages
of our glory: a hero's deed, in truth;

but more, your birth in such a strait
where you may show for our relief
the depths you plumb and from what height,
a small shed does not desire a roof.

This, great God, was not the greater feat
because of time, in that at little age
you bravely overcame the offence of ice –

worse to sweat blood than feel the cold –
but that the gap between a man and God
is wider than between a man and death.

XVI

Si ociosa no, asistió Naturaleza
incapaz a la tuya, ¡oh gran Señora!,
Concepción limpia, donde ciega ignora
lo que muda admiró de tu pureza.

Díganlo, ¡oh Virgen!, la mayor belleza
del día cuya luz tu manto dora;
la que calzas nocturna brilladora;
los que ciñen carbunclos tu cabeza.

Pura la Iglesia ya, pura te llama
la Escuela, y todo pío afecto sabio
cultas en tu favor da plumas bellas.

¿Qué mucho, pues, si aun hoy sellado el labio,
si la Naturaleza aun hoy te aclama
Virgen pura, si el Sol, Luna y estrellas?

XVI

At your conception free of stain,
great Lady, nature attended, powerless
if not idle, blindly ignorant
of your purity admired in dumbness.

Be it voiced, Virgin, by the greater beauty
of the day whose light gilds your robe,
the night's shine that shoes your feet,
the carbuncle-stones that crown your head.

Church and School call you pure,
and so, too, every wise and pious love
in handsome, learnèd scripts of your esteem.

What wonder, then, that evermore
the sealed lip, nature, the sun, moon
and stars acclaim you Virgin pure?

XVII

De pura honestidad templo sagrado,
cuyo bello cimiento y gentil muro
de blanco nácar y alabastro duro
fue por divina mano fabricado;

pequeña puerta de coral preciado,
claras lumbreras de mirar seguro,
que a la esmeralda fina el verde puro
habéis para viriles usurpado;

soberbio techo, cuyas cimbrias de oro
al claro Sol, en cuanto en torno gira,
ornan de luz, coronan de belleza;

ídolo bello, a quien humilde adoro,
oye piadoso al que por ti suspira,
tus himnos canta, y tus virtudes reza.

XVII

Sacred temple of sheer modesty,
whose handsome base and graceful wall
were masoned by some hand divine
from hard alabaster and white nacre;

narrow gate of prized coral,
bright lights of reassuring look
that, changed to monstrances, have seized
upon the pure green of the fine emerald;

proud ceiling whose beams of gold
adorn with light and crown with beauty
the lucent sun in all that wheels;

lovely idol humbly I adore:
hear him kindly who heaves sighs for you,
sings your hymns, your virtues lauds.

XVIII

En tenebrosa noche, en mar airado,
al través diera un marinero ciego,
de dulce voz, y de homicida ruego,
de Sirena mortal lisonjeado,

si el fervoroso celador cuidado
del grande Ignacio no ofreciera luego
(farol divino) su encendido fuego
a los cristales de un estanque helado.

Trueca las velas el bajel perdido,
y escollos juzga, que en la mar se lavan,
las voces que en la arena oye lascivas;

besa el puerto, altamente conducido
de las que para Norte suyo estaban
ardiendo en aguas muertas llamas vivas.

XVIII

In night's darkness, on a raging sea,
blinded, coaxed by a sweet voice,
the murderous lure of a deadly siren,
a mariner might stray off course,

were it not that the fervent, zealous
care of great Ignatius tendered
in haste to the crystals of an icy pool
a godly lamp, the self's burning blaze.

The drifting ship tacks and turns
and calculates the sea-washed reefs,
hearing the sand's lascivious voice;

she reaches port, high-guided
by living flames that in dead waters
so burned that they became her north.

XIX

Este monte, de cruces coronado,
cuya siempre dichosa excelsa cumbre,
espira luz y no vomita lumbre,
Etna glorioso, Mongibel sagrado,

trofeo es dulcemente levantado,
no ponderosa, grave pesadumbre
para oprimir sacrílega costumbre
de bando contra el cielo conjurado.

Gigantes miden sus ocultas faldas,
que a los cielos hicieron fuerza, aquella,
que los cielos padecen fuerza santa.

Sus miembros cubre y sus reliquias sella
la bien pisada tierra. Veneraldas
con tiernos ojos, con devota planta.

XIX

This mount, crowned with crosses,
exalted summit ever blest,
exhaling light, not spouting flame,
glorious Etna, sacred Mongibel,

is a trophy raised with grace
and not a heavy, crushing weight
to oppress the sacrilegious trait
of a band conspiring against heaven.

Giants who pit their strength against
the heavens – a holy strength the heavens
suffer – measure its hidden slopes.

Well-trodden earth covers their limbs
and seals up their remains; venerate them
with tender eye, with foot devout.

XX

¡Ayer deidad humana, hoy poca tierra;
aras ayer, hoy túmulo, oh mortales!
Plumas, aunque de águilas reales,
plumas son; quien lo ignora, mucho yerra.

Los miembros que hoy este sepulcro encierra,
a no estar entre aromas orientales,
mortales señas dieran de mortales;
la razón abra lo que el mármol cierra.

La Fénix que ayer Lerma fue su Arabia
es hoy entre cenizas un gusano,
y de consciencia a la persona sabia.

Si una urca se traga el ocëano,
¿qué espera un bajel luces en la gabia?
Tome tierra, que es tierra el ser humano.

XX

Yesterday's human deity, O mortals,
today's a little dust, a tomb its altars!
Imperial eagles' feathers are
feathers still: he errs who knows not such.

The limbs this tomb encloses now,
unsteeped in oriental scents,
would signal death's anguished message;
let reason open what the marble closes.

That Phoenix, Lerma its Arabia
yesterday, is now a worm amid
the ash, a conscience to the wise.

If the ocean swallow up the ship,
what hope for the boat, its mast lit up?
Let it touch earth, for earth's the human lot.

XXI

Pálida restituye a su elemento
su ya esplendor purpúreo casta rosa,
que en planta dulce un tiempo, si espinosa,
gloria del Sol, lisonja fue del viento.

El mismo que espiró süave aliento
fresca espira, marchita y siempre hermosa;
no yace, no, en la tierra, mas reposa,
negándole aun el hado lo violento.

Sus hojas sí, no su fragancia, llora
en polvo el patrio Betis, hojas bellas,
que aun en polvo el materno Tejo dora.

Ya en nuevos campos una es hoy de aquellas
flores que ilustra otra mejor aurora,
cuyo caduco aljófar son estrellas.

XXI

To its own element a chaste rose
restores its once crimson splendour;
though thorny, once it was on bush
the sun's glory, the air's caress.

Faded, though still beautiful,
it wafts its fragrance as before;
not supine on the earth, it rests, rather,
so fate spares it even ruthlessness.

Betis, its sire, does not lament
its scent, but its lovely leaves in dust;
maternal Tejo gilds them even so.

In other fields it's now a flower
a loftier dawn illuminates;
its wasted drops of dew are stars.

XXII

Máquina funeral, que desta vida
nos decís la mudanza estando queda;
pira, no de aromática arboleda,
si a más gloriosa fénix construída;

bajel en cuya gabia esclarecida
estrellas, hijas de otra mejor Leda,
serenan la Fortuna, de su rueda
la volubilidad reconocida,

farol luciente sois, que solicita
la razón, entre escollos naufragante,
al puerto; y a pesar de lo luciente,

obscura concha de una Margarita,
que, rubí en caridad, en fe diamante,
renace en nuevo Sol, en nuevo Oriente.

XXII

Funeral machine, yourself unmoving,
you tell us this life's change;
pyre, not of aromatic wood
but built to honour a more glorious phoenix;

vessel on whose illustrious main-sail
stars, children of a better Leda,
placate Fortune whose wheel's
fickleness is well known near and far;

shining beacon you are,
signalling reason to port
shipwrecked mid the shoals; despite

its shine, a pearl's dark shell,
ruby in charity, in faith diamond,
a sun reborn, an orient anew.

XXIII

Esta en forma elegante, oh peregrino,
de pórfido luciente dura llave,
el pincel niega al mundo más süave,
que dio espíritu a leño, vida a lino.

Su nombre, aun de mayor aliento dino
que en los clarines de la Fama cabe,
el campo ilustra de ese mármol grave.
Venéralo y prosigue tu camino.

Yace el Griego. Heredó Naturaleza
Arte; y el Arte, estudio. Iris, colores;
Febo, luces – si no sombras, Morfeo –.

Tanta urna, a pesar de su dureza,
lágrimas beba, y cuantos suda olores
corteza funeral de árbol sabeo.

XXIII

Here's a compact key, stranger,
whose graceful shape of glowing porphyry
deprives the world of the gentlest brush
ever gave wood soul and canvas life.

His name, worthy of more robust breath
than fills the clarions of Fame,
ennobles that earnest marble's place:
honour it and be on your way.

The Greek lies here. Nature inherited
Art; and Art, study: as Iris colours,
Phoebus lights, though Morpheus not shades.

Despite its hardness, let such an urn
drink tears, inhale the oozing scents
of the Sabaean tree's funereal bark.

XXIV

El Cuarto Enrico yace malherido
y peor muerto de plebeya mano;
el que rompió escuadrones y dio al llano
más sangre que agua Orión humedecido:

glorïoso francés; esclarecido
conducidor de ejércitos, que en vano
de lirios de oro el ya cabello cano
y de guarda real iba de ceñido.

Una temeridad astas desprecia,
una traición cuidados mil engaña,
que muros rompe en un caballo Grecia.

Archas burló el fatal cuchillo; ¡oh España,
Belona de dos mundos, fiel te precia,
y armada teme la nación extraña!

XXIV

Henry the Fourth lies sorely stabbed;
worse, a plebeian hand murdered him
who squadrons crushed and on the field
shed more blood than Orion water.

O glorious Frenchman, illustrious
leader of armies, whose hair, already
hoary, golden lilies vainly circled
and himself, too, a royal escort.

A temerity despises lances,
a treason dupes a thousand cares,
as Grecian horse breaks open walls.

A deadly knife outwitted pikestaffs.
O Spain! Bellona of two worlds, loyal,
prized; armed, feared by the foreign nation.

XXV

Sacros, altos, dorados chapiteles,
que a las nubes borráis sus arreboles,
Febo os teme por más lucientes soles,
y el Cielo por gigantes más crüeles.

Depón tus rayos, Júpiter; no celes
los tuyos, Sol; de un templo son faroles,
que al mayor mártir de los españoles
erigió el mayor rey de los fieles.

Religiosa grandeza del monarca,
cuya diestra real al nuevo mundo
abrevia, y el Oriente se le humilla.

Perdone el tiempo, lisonjee la Parca
la beldad desta Octava Maravilla,
los años deste Salomón segundo.

XXV

Sacred, towering, gilded pinnacles,
obliterating the clouds' sky-red,
as brighter suns you're feared by Phoebus,
as crueller giants you're Heaven's dread.

Jupiter, lay down your shafts; yours,
Sun, do not conceal; these are the lanterns
of a temple raised by the faithful's
greatest king to Spain's greatest martyr.

Religious grandeur of that King
whose right hand's might the New World dwarfs:
and even the Orient yields to him.

Let time forgive, the Parcae favour
the loveliness of this Eighth Wonder,
the lifetime of this Second Solomon.

XXVI

Las que a otros negó piedras Oriente,
émulas brutas del mayor lucero,
te las expone en plomo su venero,
si ya al metal no atadas más luciente;

cuanto en tu camarín pincel valiente,
bien sea natural, bien extranjero,
afecta mudo voces, y parlero
silencio en sus vocales tintas miente.

Miembros apenas dio al soplo más puro
del viento su fecunda madre bella;
Iris, pompa del Betis, sus colores;

que fuego él espirando, humo ella,
oro te muerden en su freno duro,
oh esplendor generoso de señores.

XXVI

Although not set in metal, the lead's
most lucent seam lays bare to you
those stones the East denied to others,
crude rivals of the brightest star.

Each gallant brush in your abode,
either from home or from abroad,
feigns voices; dumb itself, its tints
are the vocables of quiet's prattle.

The fertile, handsome mare bestowed
the nimblest limbs on subtlest breath,
and Iris, Betis' pomp, its hues;

the stallion breathing fire, the mare
smoke, they bite the golden bit,
you, lordliest of lords, rein them with.

XXVII

Montaña inaccesible, opuesta en vano
al atrevido paso de la gente,
(o nubes humedezcan tu alta frente,
o nieblas ciñan tu cabello cano),

Caístro el mayoral, en cuya mano
en vez de bastón vemos el tridente,
con su hermosa Silvia, Sol luciente
de rayos negros, serafín humano,

tu cerviz pisa dura; y la pastora
yugo te pone de cristal, calzada
coturnos de oro el pie, armiños vestida.

Huirá la nieve de la nieve ahora,
o ya de los dos soles desatada,
o ya de los dos blancos pies vencida.

XXVII

Forbidding mountain, vainly set
against the bold advance of man,
may clouds moisten your lofty forehead
or mists girdle your hoary hair,

herdsman Caistro – in whose hand
we see the trident, not the crook,
beside his fair Silvia, a bright sun
of black beams, human seraph – tramples

your stiff neck; and the shepherdess
in ermine clad, shod in golden buskin,
lays on you a crystal yoke.

Now the snow will flee the snow,
under the two suns thawed
or vanquished by the two white feet.

XXVIII

Hermosas damas, si la pasión ciega
no os arma de desdén, no os arma de ira,
¿quién con piedad al andaluz no mira,
y quién al andaluz su favor niega?

En el terrero, ¿quién humilde ruega,
fiel adora, idólatra suspira?
¿Quién en la plaza los bohordos tira,
mata los toros, y las cañas juega?

En los saraos, ¿quién lleva las más veces
los dulcísimos ojos de la sala,
sino galanes del Andalucía?

A ellos les dan siempre los jüeces,
en la sortija, el premio de la gala,
en el torneo, de la valentía.

XXVIII

Which of you, fair ladies, would not
kindly view the Andalusian, deny
him favour, were it not blind passion
armed you with disdain and wrath?

For on the target court, who's the humble
one to beg, in faith adore, to sigh
in idol-worship? And in the arena hurl
the spear, kill bulls, disport in jousts?

At soirées, who will bear away
from drawing-rooms the sweetest eyes,
if not some Andalusian gents?

To these the jury always gives,
in the ring, the prize of gallant dress;
in tournament, the prize of courage.

XXIX

¡Oh excelso muro, oh torres coronadas
de honor, de majestad, de gallardía!
¡Oh gran río, gran rey de Andalucía,
de arenas nobles, ya que no doradas!

¡Oh fértil llano, oh sierras levantadas,
que privilegia el cielo y dora el día!
¡Oh siempre glorïosa patria mía,
tanto por plumas cuanto por espadas!

Si entre aquellas rüinas y despojos
que enriquece Genil y Dauro baña
tu memoria no fue alimento mío,

nunca merezcan mis ausentes ojos
ver tu muro, tus torres y tu río,
tu llano y sierra, ¡oh patria, oh flor de España!

XXIX

Exalted walls, battlements crowned
with honour, courage, majesty!
Great river! Great king of Andalusia,
of noble if not golden sands!

O fertile plains, O high sierras
which heaven favours and day gilds!
O my hometown forever glorious
with pen no less than with the sword!

If mid those ruins and spoils enriched
by Genil, lapped by Dauro, your memory
cease to be my sustenance,

never may my distant eyes behold
your walls, battlements, rivers, plain,
O my hometown, O flower of Spain!

XXX

¡Oh niebla del estado más sereno,
furia infernal, serpiente mal nacida!
¡Oh ponzoñosa víbora, escondida
de verde prado en oloroso seno!

¡Oh entre el néctar de amor mortal veneno
que en vaso de cristal quitas la vida!
¡Oh espada, sobre mí de un pelo asida,
de la amorosa espuela duro freno!

¡Oh celo, del favor verdugo eterno!
vuélvete al lugar triste donde estabas
O al reino (si allá cabes) del espanto.

Mas no cabrás allá, que pues ha tanto
que comes de ti mesmo y no te acabas,
mayor debes de ser que el mismo infierno.

XXX

O mist of most benignant weather,
infernal rage, perfidious snake!
O venomous viper hiding in
a green field's fragrant lap!

A deadly poison in love's nectar,
snatching life out of a crystal cup!
A sword that hangs above me by a hair,
a hard bridle to the amorous spur!

O jealousy, grace's eternal hangman!
Return to that sad place wherein you lived,
or to the realm of fright, if you fit there.

But you won't fit; for you
have eaten of yourself so much
you must be larger now than even hell.

XXXI

Ya besando unas manos cristalinas,
ya anudándome a un blanco y liso cuello,
ya esparciendo por él aquel cabello
que Amor sacó entre el oro de sus minas,

ya quebrando en aquellas perlas finas
palabras dulces mil sin merecello,
ya cogiendo de cada labio bello
purpúreas rosas sin temor de espinas,

estaba, oh claro sol invidïoso,
cuando tu luz, hiriéndome los ojos,
mató mi gloria y acabó mi suerte.

Si el cielo ya no es menos poderoso,
porque no den los tuyos más enojos,
rayos, como a tu hijo, te den muerte.

XXXI

Now kissing hands of crystal clearness,
clasping now a white smooth neck,
or spreading over it that hair
dug up in gold by Love out of its mines;

now pressing through those fine pearls
a thousand sweet, unmerited words,
or gathering out of every pretty lip
scarlet roses unafraid of thorns,

thus I was, bright and envious sun,
when your light, wounding these eyes of mine,
killed my light and finished off my luck.

If heaven's power has not decreased,
let lightning shafts bring death on you
as on your son, and cause no further rage.

XXXII

No de fino diamante, o rubí ardiente
(luces brillando aquél, éste centellas),
crespo volumen vio de plumas bellas
nacer la gala más vistosamente,

que, oscura el vuelo, y con razón doliente,
de la perla católica, que sellas,
a besar te levantas las estrellas,
melancólica aguja, si luciente.

Pompa eres de dolor, seña no vana
de nuestra vanidad, dígalo el viento,
que ya de luces, ya de aromas tanto

humo te debe. ¡Ay ambición humana,
prudente pavón hoy con ojos ciento,
si al desengaño se los das, y al llanto!

XXXII

The plume's proud finery had scarcely seen
so crisp a mass of glowing ruby
or pure diamond, one casting beams,
the other sparks, more grandly rise,

when with dark and rightly doleful flight,
despondent though bright spire,
you rise upwards to kiss the stars
of the Catholic pearl you seal.

You're sorrow's pomp, no vain sign
of our vanity, let the wind speak
which owes you so much smoke of lights

or scents. O man's wretched ambition,
wise peacock now, your hundred eyes,
given to undeceit and plaint!

XXXIII

Al tronco descansaba de una encina
que invidia de los bosques fue lozana,
cuando segur legal una mañana
alto horror me dejó con su rüina.

Laurel que de sus ramas hizo dina
mi lira, ruda sí, mas castellana,
hierro luego fatal su pompa vana
(culpa tuya, Calíope) fulmina.

En verdes hojas como el de Minerva
árbol culto, del Sol yace abrasado,
aljófar, sus cenizas, de la yerba.

¡Cuánta esperanza miente a un desdichado!
¿A qué más desengaños me reserva,
a qué escarmientos me vincula el hado?

XXXIII

By an ilex tree I used to rest,
its loveliness the envy of all woods;
when the law's axe ravaged it
one day, it caused me utter grief.

Fatal iron's lightning flash
(your fault, Calliope) strikes
the proud pomp of a laurel that made my lyre,
coarse but Castilian, worthy of its boughs.

Minerva's learnèd tree, its green
leaves hoary-headed, lies sun-shrivelled,
the grass besprinkled with its ash.

What hope deceives a hapless one?
For what distress am I withheld
by Fate, to what chastisement bound?

XXXIV

Verdes juncos del Duero a mi pastora
tejieron dulce generosa cuna;
blancas palmas, si el Tajo tiene alguna,
cubren su pastoral albergue ahora.

Los montes mide y las campañas mora
flechando una dorada media luna,
cual dicen que a las fieras fue importuna
del Eurota la casta cazadora.

De un blanco armiño el esplendor vestida,
los blancos pies distinguen de la nieve
los coturnos que calza esta homicida;

bien tal, pues montaraz y endurecida,
contra las fieras sólo un arco mueve,
y dos arcos tendió contra mi vida.

XXXIV

Green rushes of the Duero wove
my shepherdess's sweet and noble cot;
white palms, if Tajo any has,
now thatch her shepherd's rustic hut.

She roams the hills, she dwells on plains,
shooting a half-moon golden-stained,
just as, they say, the chaste huntress
harried the wild beasts of Eurotas.

Garbed in the splendour of white ermine,
this murderess is shod in buskins
which tell her feet apart from snow;

truly a wild and hardened murderess,
she points at the wild beasts one bow,
but against my life she points two.

XXXV

Cual parece al romper de la mañana
aljófar blanco sobre frescas rosas,
o cual por manos hecha, artificiosas,
bordadura de perlas sobre grana,

tales de mi pastora soberana
parecían las lágrimas hermosas
sobre las dos mejillas milagrosas,
de quien mezcladas sangre y leche mana,

lanzando a vueltas de su tierno llanto
un ardiente suspiro de su pecho,
tal que el más duro canto enterneciera,

si enternecer bastara un duro canto,
mirad qué habrá con un corazón hecho,
que al llanto y al suspiro fue de cera.

XXXV

Just as at break of day white dew
appears upon cool roses, or as
embroidery of pearls, of skilful craft,
would show against a crimson cloth,

just so the lovely tears upon
the marvellous cheeks of my fair
shepherdess, from which both blood
and milk together mixed outpoured,

when, her tender plaint renewed,
an ardent sigh then left her breast
such as would soften hardest stone:

if obdurate stone she could make yield,
just think how she has wrought a heart
already wax to tears and sighs.

XXXVI

Al tramontar del sol, la ninfa mía,
de flores despojando el verde llano,
cuantas troncaba la hermosa mano,
tantas el blanco pie crecer hacía.

Ondeábale el viento que corría
el oro fino con error galano,
cual verde hoja de álamo lozano
se mueve al rojo despuntar del día.

Mas luego que ciñó sus sienes bellas
de los varios despojos de su falda
(término puesto al oro y a la nieve),

juraré que lució más su guirnalda
con ser de flores, la otra ser de estrellas,
que la que ilustra el cielo en luces nueve.

XXXVI

In daylight while the nymph I love
despoiled the green plain of flowers,
with her white foot she made as many
grow as her fair hand had plucked.

The wind that blew ruffled
with gallant error her gold array
as a lush poplar's green leaf
stirs at the red dawn of day.

But once she'd girt her handsome brow
with her skirt's various spoils
(a border set to gold and snow),

I'll swear her wreath shone brighter
though of flowers, not stars, than that
emblazing heaven in its nine lights.

XXXVII

En el cristal de tu divina mano
de Amor bebí el dulcísimo veneno,
néctar ardiente que me abrasa el seno,
y templar con la ausencia pensé en vano.

Tal, Claudia bella, del rapaz tirano
es arpón de oro tu mirar sereno,
que cuanto más ausente dél, más peno,
de sus golpes el pecho menos sano.

Tus cadenas al pie, lloro al rüido
de un eslabón y otro mi destierro,
más desviado, pero más perdido,

¿Cuándo será aquel día que por yerro,
oh, serafín, desates, bien nacido,
con manos de cristal nudos de hierro?

XXXVII

From your divine hand's crystal I drank
love's sweetest poison, burning nectar
that inflames my breast I thought
in vain with absence I could temper.

Your calm gaze, fair Claudia, to such degree's
the gold harpoon of that tyrannous child,
the further off I go, the more I pine,
my breast less mended of its strokes.

Foot-fettered in your chains, I moan
to their rings' clank my banishment,
ever more distant, yet still more lost.

When shall come the day, noble seraph,
you will mistakenly untie
with crystal hands these iron knots?

XXXVIII

Prisión del nácar era articulado,
de mi firmeza un émulo luciente,
un dïamante, ingenïosamente
en oro también él aprisionado.

Clori, pues, que su dedo apremïado
de metal aun precioso no consiente,
gallarda un día, sobre impacïente,
lo redimió del vínculo dorado.

Mas, ay, que insidïoso latón breve
de los cristales de su bella mano
sacrílego divina sangre bebe:

púrpura ilustró menos indïano
marfil; invidïosa, sobre nieve,
claveles deshojó la Aurora en vano.

XXXVIII

To the jointed nacre it was a jail,
a shining rival to my steadfastness,
a diamond it, too, imprisoned
with ingenuity in gold.

Clori, then, dissenting that
her finger should be pressed by metal
however fine, one day, brave, impatient,
relieved it of its golden bond.

But, alas, insidious tiny tin
drinks, in sacrilege, divine blood
from the crystals of her lovely hand:

never did scarlet so point up
Indian ivory; in envy but in vain
dawn plucked pink petals on the snow.

XXXIX

Cosas, Celalba mía, he visto extrañas:
cascarse nubes, desbocarse vientos,
altas torres besar sus fundamentos,
y vomitar la tierra sus entrañas;

duras puentes romper, cual tiernas cañas,
arroyos prodigiosos, ríos violentos,
mal vadeados de los pensamientos,
y enfrenados peor de las montañas;

los días de Noé, gentes subidas
a los más altos pinos levantados,
en las robustas hayas más crecidas.

Pastores, perros, chozas y ganados
sobre las aguas vi, sin forma y vidas,
y nada temí más que mis cuidados.

XXXIX

Strange things I've seen, Celalba:
clashing of clouds, bolting winds,
tall towers kiss their foundation,
the earth spew up its very guts;

prodigious creeks breaking stout bridges
as though thin reeds, tumultuous streams
forded ill by thoughts, and held
by mountains with even greater pains;

days of Noah, people clambering up
the tallest pines that ever soared,
the sturdiest beeches that ever grew.

Shepherds, dogs, cabins, herds
I saw on the waters, and formless life,
and I feared naught more than my cares.

XL

Descaminado, enfermo, peregrino,
en tenebrosa noche, con pie incierto,
la confusión pisando del desierto,
voces en vano dio, pasos sin tino.

Repetido latir, si no vecino,
distincto oyó de can siempre despierto,
y en pastoral albergue mal cubierto
piedad halló, si no halló camino.

Salió el Sol, y entre armiños escondida,
soñolienta beldad con dulce saña
salteó al no bien sano pasajero.

Pagará el hospedaje con la vida;
más le valiera errar en la montaña
que morir de la suerte que yo muero.

XL

Astray and sick and wandering,
in gloomy night, with unsure foot,
treading the desert's sandy maze,
in vain he shouted, took aimless step.

He heard the ever-wakeful hound's
persistent barking, faraway,
and in a shepherd's ill-roofed hut
compassion found, though not a route.

The sun came out, and a sleepy beauty,
hid in ermines, beset with gentle rage
the unrecuperated traveller.

His lodging-bill will be his life;
would that he choose to roam the hills
rather than die the way I die.

XLI

Yacen aquí los huesos sepultados
de una amistad que al mundo será una,
o ya para experiencia de fortuna,
o ya para escarmiento de cuidados.

Nació entre pensamientos, aunque honrados,
grave al amor, a muchos importuna;
tanto que la mataron en la cuna
ojos de invidia y de ponzoña armados.

Breve urna los sella como huesos,
al fin, de malograda criatura;
pero versos los honran inmortales,

que vivirán en el sepulcro impresos,
siendo la piedra Felixmena dura,
Daliso el escultor, cincel sus males.

XLI

Herein lie entombed the bones of such
a friendship the world has rarely seen,
whether as a trial of luck
or as a caution to love's toils.

Born mid upright thoughts that yet
weigh down on love, a chafe to many,
it angered eyes, with spite and envy
armed, so that they killed it in its cot.

A small urn encloses them as bones
of the mishap's child they were; but they
are honoured by immortal verse

that shall persist in lettered tomb,
Felixmena, the hard stone,
Daliso the sculptor, their ills the chisel.

XLII

La dulce boca que a gustar convida
un humor entre perlas distilado
y a no invidiar aquel licor sagrado
que a Júpiter ministra el garzón de Ida,

amantes, no toquéis, si queréis vida;
porque entre un labio y otro colorado
Amor está, de su veneno armado,
cual entre flor y flor sierpe escondida.

No os engañen las rosas, que a la Aurora
diréis que, aljofaradas y olorosas,
se le cayeron del purpúreo seno;

manzanas son de Tántalo, y no rosas,
que después huyen del que incitan hora
y sólo del Amor queda el veneno.

XLII

If, lovers, you love life, don't touch
the sweet mouth tempting you to taste
the moisture issuing from mid pearls,
to turn from envy of the sacred drink

that's poured by Ida's youth to Jove;
for between two ruddy lips
love lies ready with poison tip
like a serpent hidden away in flowers.

Be undeceived by roses you will say
fell dew-spangled and perfumed
out of the crimson bosom of the dawn;

apples of Tantalus, not roses,
they flee from him they now entice
so that alone love's poison stays.

XLIII

Si Amor entre las plumas de su nido
prendió mi libertad, ¿qué hará ahora,
que en tus ojos, dulcísma señora,
armado vuela, ya que no vestido?

Entre las vïoletas fui herido
del áspid que hoy entre los lilios mora,
igual fuerza tenías siendo aurora,
que ya como sol tienes bien nacido.

Saludaré tu luz con voz doliente,
cual tierno ruiseñor en prisión dura
despide quejas, pero dulcemente.

Diré cómo de rayos vi tu frente
coronada, y que hace tu hermosura
cantar las aves, y llorar la gente.

XLIII

If Love still nesting in its plumes
could seize my liberty, what now,
undressed yet armed, sweetest lady,
will it do flying in your eyes?

The asp that lies in lilies now,
in violets once did me harm,
for you at dawn had equal strength
as sun that reached meridian.

I'll greet the light with saddened voice
as gentle nightingale in its hard cell
dispatches moans, however sweet.

I'll tell how I saw rays crowning
your head, and how your loveliness
compels the birds to sing and folk to cry.

XLIV

Suspiros tristes, lágrimas cansadas,
que lanza el corazón, los ojos llueven,
los troncos bañan y las ramas mueven
de estas plantas, a Alcides consagradas;

mas del viento las fuerzas conjuradas
los suspiros desatan y remueven,
y los troncos las lágrimas se beben,
mal ellos y peor ellas derramadas.

Hasta en mi tierno rostro aquel tributo
que dan mis ojos, invisible mano
de sombra o de aire me la deja enjuto,

porque aquel ángel fieramente humano
no crea mi dolor, y así es mi fruto
llorar sin premio y suspirar en vano.

XLIV

Sad sighs of my expressive heart,
wearied tears that my eyes shed,
wash the trunks and shake the boughs
of these woods to Alcides vowed;

but sighs unleash and agitate
the wind's conspiratorial rage,
and the trees drink the tears, unsoothing
draught that was not poured to sate.

An invisible hand of shadow and air
wipes out, even upon my tender
face, the tribute my eyes give,

so that that fiercely human angel
may not believe my grief, and thus my harvest
is to weep rewardless, sigh in vain.

XLV

Ni en este monte, este aire, ni este río
corre fiera, vuela ave, pece nada,
de quien con atención no sea escuchada
la triste voz del triste llanto mío;

y aunque en la fuerza sea del estío
al viento mi querella encomendada,
cuando a cada cual de ellos más le agrada
fresca cueva, árbol verde, arroyo frío,

a compasión movidos de mi llanto,
dejan la sombra, el ramo y la hondura,
cual ya por escuchar el dulce canto

de aquel que, de Strimón en la espesura,
los suspendía cien mil veces. ¡Tanto
puede mi mal, y pudo su dulzura!

XLV

No wild beast runs, bird flies, fish swims
upon this hill, this air, this stream,
that will not hear attentively
the sad voice of my sad plaint;

and though my plea's entrusted to
the wind at height of summer heat,
when a cool cave, a bough, a stream
most pleases each and all of them,

they're moved to pity by my groan,
and leave the shade, the bough, the deep
as once they did to hear the sweet song

of him who in the tanglewood
of Strymo a thousand times charmed them.
As much my ill can do, its sweetness can.

XLVI

¡Oh claro honor del líquido elemento,
dulce arroyuelo de corriente plata,
cuya agua entre la yerba se dilata
con regalado son, con paso lento!,

pues la por quien helar y arder me siento,
(mientras en ti se mira), Amor retrata
de su rostro la nieve y la escarlata
en tu tranquilo y blando movimiento,

vete como te vas; no dejes floja
la undosa rienda al cristalino freno
con que gobiernas tu veloz corriente;

que no es bien que confusamente acoja
tanta belleza en su profundo seno
el gran señor del húmido tridente.

XLVI

Bright glory of the liquid element,
sweet rivulet of flowing silver
whose waters through the meadow course
with gentle sound and easy pace!

While looking at herself in you,
love paints in your soft quiet motion
the snow and scarlet of the face
of her for whom I burn and freeze;

move as you do; do not let go
the crystal bit's sinuous rein
with which you drive your racing flow;

for it's unfit, the great lord
of the wet trident in his deep bosom
should receive a shattered loveliness.

XLVII

Gallardas plantas, que con voz doliente,
al osado Faetón llorastes vivas,
y ya sin invidiar palmas ni olivas,
muertas podéis ceñir cualquiera frente.

Así del sol estivo al rayo ardiente,
blanco coro de náyades lascivas,
precie más vuestras sombras fugitivas,
que verde margen de escondida fuente.

Y así bese (a pesar del seco estío)
vuestros troncos (ya un tiempo pies humanos)
el raudo curso deste undoso río;

que lloréis (pues llorar sólo a vos toca
locas empresas, ardimientos vanos)
mi ardimiento en amar, mi empresa loca.

XLVII

Graceful plants, you who, living,
mourned daring Phaëton, and, now dead,
unenvious of the palm or olive,
may form a wreath for any forehead;

as a white chorus of sensual naiads
under the summer sun's burning rays
will more esteem your fleeting shades
than the green bank of a hidden spring,

and as the wavy river's rapid course,
despite the summer's drought, will kiss
your trunks that once were human feet,

so weep you now – to weep is your
sole lot – for wild ventures, vain ardours,
my ardent loving, my wild venture.

XLVIII

En este occidental, en este, oh Licio,
climatérico lustro de tu vida,
todo mal afirmado pie es caída,
toda fácil caída es precipicio.

¿Caduca el paso? Ilústrese el jüicio.
Desátandose va la tierra unida;
¿qué prudencia, del polvo prevenida,
la rüina aguardó del edificio?

La piel no sólo, sierpe venenosa,
mas con la piel los años se desnuda,
y el hombre no. ¡Ciego discurso humano!

¡Oh aquel dichoso, que la ponderosa
porción depuesta en una piedra muda,
la leve da al zafiro soberano!

XLVIII

At this declining, climacteric
stage of your career, Licio,
every ill-placed foot's a fall,
every easy fall a precipice.

Does footstep fail? Let judgement show.
The bonded clay is crumbling.
What prudence, warned by sift of sand,
delayed until the structure fell?

The venomous snake sloughs not only
skin, but with its skin the years;
not so man. Blind human reason!

Happy the man who, his heavy share
disposed beneath mute stone, entrusts
to sovereign sapphire his light self!

XLVIX

Mientras por competir con tu cabello,
oro bruñido al sol relumbra en vano;
mientras con menosprecio en medio el llano
mira tu blanca frente el lilio bello;

mientras a cada labio, por cogello,
siguen más ojos que al clavel temprano,
y mientras triunfa con desdén lozano
del luciente cristal tu gentil cuello;

goza cuello, cabello, labio y frente,
antes que lo que fue en tu edad dorada
oro, lilio, clavel, cristal luciente,

no sólo en plata o víola troncada
se vuelva, mas tú y ello juntamente
en tierra, en humo, en polvo, en sombra, en nada.

XLVIX

While burnished gold shines vainly
in the sun, a rival to your hair,
while your white forehead spitefully
regards the fields' fair lily;

while more eyes seek each lip of yours
than look to find the early carnation,
and while your stately neck with proud
disdain conquers shining crystal,

enjoy neck, hair, lip and forehead,
before what years of glory made
gold, lily, carnation, shining crystal,

not only turns to silver or lopped pansy,
but it and you together turn
to clay, smoke, dust, shadow, naught.

L

Menos solicitó veloz saeta
destinada señal, que mordió aguda;
agonal carro por la arena muda
no coronó con más silencio meta,

que presurosa corre, que secreta
a su fin nuestra edad. A quien lo duda,
(fiera que sea de razón desnuda)
cada sol repetido es un cometa.

Confiésalo Cartago, ¿y tú lo ignoras?
Peligro corres, Licio, si porfías
en seguir sombras y abrazar engaños.

Mal te perdonarán a ti las horas,
las horas que limando están los días,
los días que royendo están los años.

L

A hurtling arrow biting sharp
its predetermined mark, asks less;
across the silent sand no chariot
ends its course with greater quiet

than our fleeting, secret time hastens
to its close. To him who doubts,
a beast deprived of reason,
repeated suns are but a comet.

Will Carthage reck and you not know?
You'd run a risk, Licio, to contend
in chasing shades, embracing lies.

The hours will little spare your life,
the hours that file away your days,
the days that gnaw away your years.

LI

Herido el blanco pie del hierro breve,
saludable si agudo, amiga mía,
mi rostro tiñes de melancolia,
mientras de rosicler tiñes la nieve.

Temo (que quien bien ama, temer debe)
el triste fin de la que perdió el día,
en roja sangre y en ponzoña fría
bañando el pie que descuidado mueve.

Temo aquel fin, porque el remedio para,
si no me presta el sonoroso Orfeo
con su instrumento dulce su voz clara.

¡Mas ay, que cuando no mi lira, creo
que mil veces mi voz te revocara,
y otras mil te perdiera mi deseo!

LI

As the short weapon, sharp though healing,
strikes your white foot, you tint with gloom,
darling, my countenance, while yet
you dye the snow with rosy pink.

I dread, as anyone should that loves,
the mournful fate of her who lost
daylight, the unheeding foot she swung
red-bathed in blood and poison-chilled.

I dread that fate because its cure would cease
should sonorous Orpheus rob me
of his noble voice and gentle strings.

But ah, were my lyre dumb, I know my voice
would call you back a thousand times,
and just as often my desire would lose you.

Appendices

Góngora's Defence of Poetic Obscurity

'For a black lady's sake ...'
(attributed to Góngora)

Defensa de la oscuridad poética

De una carta de Góngora, Córdoba, septiembre de 1615

... y si la oscuridad y estilo entricado de Ovidio (que en lo *de Ponto* y en lo *de Tristibus* fue tan claro como se ve, y tan obscuro en las *Transformaciones* [Metamorfosis]), da causa a que, vacilando el entendimiento en fuerza de discurso, trabajándole (pues crece con cualquier acto de valor), alcance lo que así en la lectura superficial de sus versos no pudo entender, luego hase de confesar que tiene utilidad avivar el ingenio, y eso nació de la oscuridad del poeta. Eso mismo hallará V.m. en mis *Soledades*, si tiene capacidad para quitar la corteza y descubrir lo misterioso que encubren. De honroso, en dos maneras considero que me ha sido honrosa esta poesía: si entendida para los doctos, causarme ha autoridad, siendo lance forzoso venerar que nuestra lengua a costa de mi trabajo haya llegado a la perfección y alteza de la latina. [...] Demás que honra me ha causado hacerme escuro a los ignorantes, que esa es la distinción de los hombres doctos, hablar de manera que a ellos les parezca griego; pues no se han de dar las piedras preciosas a animales de cerda. [...] Deleitable tiene lo que en los dos puntos de arriba queda explicado, pues si deleitar el entendimiento es darle razones que le concluyan y se midan con su contento, descubriendo lo que está debajo de esos tropos, por fuerza el entendimiento ha de quedar convencido, y convencido, satisfecho; demás que, como el fin del entendimiento es hacer presa en verdades, que por eso no le satisface nada, si no es la primera verdad, conforme a aquella sentencia de san Agustín: *Inquietum est cor nostrum, donec requiescat in te*, en tanto quedará más deleitado, cuanto, obligándole a la especulación por la obscuridad de la obra, fuera hallando debajo de las sombras asimilaciones a su concepto...

Góngora's Defence of Poetic Obscurity

From a letter by Góngora, Córdoba, September 1615

... and if the obscurity and intricate style of Ovid (so clear in the material from the *Black Sea* ('Epistolae ex Ponto') and the *Lamentations* ('Tristia'), but in the *Metamorphoses* so obscure) occasions the intellect, that wavers for tough reasoning, to reach through exercise (since it thrives by being challenged) what a mere reading of the verse would not attain, then one must own that ingenuity is thereby enhanced, which goes back to the poet's obscurity. You will find as much in my *Soledades* once you have removed the rind and bared the secret they conceal. As to prestige, I deem twofold the honour this poetry does me: if the learned come by it, they must needs credit me with the painstaking endeavour of carrying our language to the accomplishment and heights of Latin. [...] Being obscure to the ignorant honours me as well, for what to these will sound like Greek is only refinement in educated men. You do not waste precious stones on swine. [...] Both these considerations bespeak enjoyment, since you please the intellect by feeding it reasons that answer and content it, revealing what lies behind the figures so that it is perforce overcome by the weight of persuasion; then again, the intellect is aimed at grasping truth, which is why nothing if not Prime Truth gives it rest, as stated by Saint Augustine, 'Restless is our heart till it rests in Thee.' Enjoyment then which shall be the greater when the intellect, compelled to ponder by the piece's obscurity, retrieves one by one, as if out of the shadows, the reflections of its very notions ...

Por una negra señora...

Por una negra señora
un negro galán doliente
negras lágrimas derrama
de un negro pecho que tiene.

Lleva una negra guitarra,
negras las cuerdas y verdes,
negras también las clavijas
por ser negro quien las tuerce.

Hablole una negra noche,
y tan negra que parece
que de su negra pasión
el negro luto le viene:

«¡Negras pascuas me de Dios,
si más negro no me tienen
los negros amores tuyos
que el negro color de allende!

Un negro favor te pido,
si negros favores vendes,
y si con favores negros
un negro pagarse debe.»

La negra señora entonces,
enfadada del negrete,
con estas negras razones
al galán negro entristece:

«Vaya muy enhoranegra
el negro que tal pretende,
pues para galanes negros
se hicieron negros desdenes.»

For a black lady's sake ...

For a black lady's sake
a grieving black lover
sheds jet-black tears
out of his black passion.

He carries a black guitar,
black and green its strings,
black, too, its tuning-pegs,
since black is their tuner.

On a black night he spoke,
so black that it seemed
that from its black passion
came his black grief.

'God grant me black times
if these your black loves,
don't keep me blacker
than the black colour.

Your black gift I seek
if black gifts you sell,
if black gifts requite
a black gentleman.'

Then the black lady
whom the black gent annoys
saddens the black gallant
with this black report:

'Be off and let blackness
befall the black suitor;
rebuttals are black,
were meant for black lovers.'

El negro señor entonces,
no queriendo ennegrecerse
más de lo negro, quitose
el negro sombrero y fuese.

At that, the black gent
who desired to be blackened
no further than blackness,
doffed his black hat and left.

Notes

GÓNGORA'S POETRY has been heavily annotated by scholars, and no doubt such annotations have their usefulness and even necessity for the student. The purpose of this little book, however, is not pedagogic but to present a small selection of Góngora's shorter poems to English-speaking readers with minimum distraction from the poems themselves. The few notes that follow are not scholarly, but merely bits and pieces which the translator gleaned from friends and various reading as he worked on the texts; their inclusion here is solely for the sake of the more curious reader who may desire some idea of the kind of material with which Góngora was accustomed to work.

I   The reign of night, the religious darkness and cruelty of the pre-Christian world. Note the imagery of temporal power: 'sway', 'reigned', 'diadem', 'kingdom'.

> For, while all things were in quiet silence and
> the night was in the midst of her course,
> The almighty word leapt down from heaven ...
>   – Wisdom 18:14–15

The Virgin is the dawn light preceding and reflecting the rising sun that is Jesus.

It is Catholic teaching that Mary gave birth to Christ without ceasing to be a virgin.

It was the humble ('the hay') of the world – Mary, Joseph, the Magi, the Shepherds, not the proud – Herod – who were 'true' to Christ.

The infant Jesus survived Herod's attempts ('many snows') to kill him.

carnation: Christ.
the bosom of dawn: Mary was 'found with child, of the Holy Ghost' (Matthew 1:18)
the hay: humanity / flesh. Isaiah 40:6.

149

II Christ is both the good shepherd and, in the form of the Eucharist, the sustaining food of his flock.

As Dámaso Alonso has observed, there are many parallels in Christian devotional literature to Góngora's cross as a tree on which a shepherd has been raised by love; for example, these lines from San Juan de la Cruz's 'El pastorcico':

> *Y a cabo de un gran rato se ha encumbrado*
> *sobre un árbol do abrió sus brazos bellos,*
> *y muerto se ha quedado, asido de ellos,*
> *el pecho del amor muy lastimado.*

> (And he has at great length climbed
> upon a tree, there to stretch out his lovely arms,
> and held by them lifeless he lies,
> his breast much hurt by love.)

III In this ballad a *forzado*, that is to say, a captive Christian compelled to serve at the oars, who is serving on a galley of Dragut (a famous Turkish pirate of the sixteenth century), as the ship passes close to the Spanish coast, calls on the sea to give him news of his wife.

The South Sea, *el mar del Sur*, was how the Pacific Ocean was known. It was associated with beautiful pearls; hence Góngora develops his conceit of the wife's tears that fall into the sea, as pearls more beautiful than (and thus surpassing) those of the South Sea.

the water has tongues: a strip of land jutting into the sea is described in Spanish as *lengua de tierra*; also an inlet of sea cutting into land is described as *lengua de agua*.
the Order: the crusading Order of Malta.
the oarsmate: the master of the galley-slaves.

VI This ballad is addressed to a jealous girl who has not been well treated by her lover. Blue is the symbolic colour of jealousy.

In Góngora's idiom *niña* connotes the unmarried state (*virgo intacta*) whether of young girl or older woman. It would be a stylistic error to translate *niña* literally as 'child' as the poem contains no hint of the paternalism that would accompany the word 'child' in English.

VIII This poem is in the tradition of *alboradas*, lyrics of dawn trysts.

At one level the refrain can be read as a conventional evocation of dawn. It employs the traditional elements of the dawn landscape: nightingales, flowers and streams. In popular *alboradas*, sunrise is often marked by the ringing of bells and sometimes by a military reveille that parts soldiers from their loved ones. The refrain also draws on the tradition of serenading the dawn with musical instruments. At another level, the refrain may refer to the poet's awakening mistress whose eyes are the 'suns' he adores, the curls of her hair are 'the tiny golden trumpets', her tears of parting 'the little silver bells'. If this second reading is valid, then the music that greets the sunrise is not only that of the buzzing bees and the coursing streams, but also the lady's tears of parting.

The poet and his mistress are roused to love by the siren voices of the dawn chorus; additionally, the poet is aroused to love by the tears and the beauty of his mistress (the *un*plumaged siren).

The second stanza contains the enigmatic meaning of the other 'instrument'. Is this another bird of dawn, or is it the poet's mistress whose tears and beauty create a music that appeals not to the ear, but to the spirit?

The 'two lovely streams' are the coursing stream and the bees buzzing over the jasmines, the conventional music of the *alborada*; but perhaps there is also another level of meaning, which is that the poet's mistress is wearing the jasmines in her hair, and that her flowing hair and her tears are two streams of an enthralling music that arouses them to love.

My thanks to Terry O'Reilly of University College, Cork, for help with this poem.

X Góngora represents the river Po, which served as Phaëton's tomb when he fell from the heavens having attempted to steer the horses of the Sun (his father), as enraged because the Conde de Villamediana, Góngora's patron and friend, in his *Fábula de Faetón*, had created an immortal monument, superior to that of the river. For the story of Phaëton, see the note on XLVII.

XIII The image here is of two bright eyes, black eyelids, blonde hair, the face like heaven, a Venus.

My thanks to Sr Antonio Carreira of Madrid for generously supplying me with a variant text of the Spanish. To avoid, however, dealing with textual matters beyond my competence I have chosen to adhere to a single reputable text.

XV The heroism of the crucified Christ paradoxically lies in Christ's passivity. Probably without due cause, I am nonetheless reminded by Góngora's first quartet of the Old English poetic fragment 'The Vision of the Cross' in which the unknown poet, employing the conventions of epic verse, resolves the technical difficulty of Christ's passive heroism by personifying the cross and transferring to it the function of expressing the passive aspect of the Crucifixion, projecting Christ as the active agent that the epic conventions demanded.

The main point of Góngora's poem is that God, by becoming man in Christ, achieved an act of heroism superior to any notion of heroism deriving from the chivalric code which supplies the poem's conventions.

offence of ice: the winter of Christ's birth.

XVI 'And there appeared a great wonder in heaven; a woman clothed with the sun, and the moon under her feet, and upon her head a crown of twelve stars.' – Revelation 12:1

free of stain: according to Catholic dogma, Mary alone of the children of Adam was preserved immune, through the merits of her Son, from the *stain* of Original Sin.

nature: although nature is *powerless* to perform such a portent (i.e. the Immaculate Conception), it does not remain idle, but provides what theologians have called *potentia activa*, a kind of readiness. Sanctifying grace is by essence beyond nature, yet it can be 'infused' in nature: although nature, in its *dumbness*, cannot know (i.e. is *blindly ignorant* of) grace, it can nonetheless respond with awe (*admire*) when 'infused' with grace by God.

XVII Petrarch's influence is clearly evident in this sonnet, though Salcedo Coronel has apparently traced the influence of a sonnet by Minturno.

In the Bible and in the Christian mystics, the attributes of divine love are often expressed symbolically in terms of human love. While highly conscious of this tradition, Góngora is working at the same time within the Petrarchan literary conventions, displaying his masterly control of the medium by the calculated daring of line 12.

In most Catholic Prayer Books, one may find the Litany of the Blessed Virgin, which contains invocations relevant to Góngora's sonnet: 'tower of ivory', 'house of gold', 'gate of Heaven'.

21:9 ff. of Revelation symbolically portray the 'Spouse of the Lamb'. While these verses actually refer to the community of the faithful, they have also been applied to the Virgin Mary:

> ... and her light was like unto a stone most precious, even like a jasper stone, clear as crystal. [9]
>
> And the building of the wall of it was of jasper; and the city was pure gold, like unto a clear glass. [18]
>
> And the foundations of the wall of the city were garnished with all manner of precious stones. The first foundation was jasper; the second, sapphire; the third, a chalcedony; the fourth, an emerald. [19]

XVIII On this poem Gracián comments: '... a graceful and interesting sonnet to the Patriarch Saint Ignatius who plunged ... into a freezing pool in order to assuage the fire of a youth's lasciviousness.' Although no ascetic, Góngora's admiration for the stern discipline of his fellow Spaniard is clearly evident.

	Italics of the last line in Spanish: it was customary for poets in Góngora's time to engage in poetic competitions, one of which was to build a poem on a given line, in this case, the last line in italics.
XIX	The poem's second quartet contrasts the Christian hermits who lived and were buried on a mountain in Granada, called Sacro Monte (the Mongibel of the poem, as though it were a Vulcan of the spirit), with the mythical Titans who assaulted the heavens. This mountain, then, is a trophy of spiritual struggle, not a weight to crush the rebellious; it is raised, not in volcanic anger, like a punishment, but with gentleness, as a reward.

The sextet alludes to the burial places of the hermits, spiritual giants, on the slopes of the mountain; and it refers to a passage in the Gospels where Jesus says that heaven yields only to the strong. |
| XX | On the tomb of the Duquesa de Lerma.

The first stanza of the famous dirge from *The Contention of Ajax and Ulysses* by James Shirley (1596–1666), provides an excellent gloss on Góngora's sonnet:

> The glories of our blood and state
>   Are shadows, not substantial things;
> There is no armour against fate;
> Death lays his icy hand on kings:
>   Sceptre and crown
>   Must tumble down,
> And in the dust be equal made
> With the poor crooked scythe and spade.

Imperial eagles' feathers: nobility. |
| XXI | The kind of play with conceits which Góngora employs in this poem can perhaps best be conveyed to the reader of English poetry by a quotation from George Herbert's 'Life':

> Farewell, dear flowers; sweetly your time
>   [ye spent,
>   Fit, while ye lived, for smell or ornament,
>   And after death for cures. |

> I follow straight, without complaints or grief;
> Since, if my scent be good, I care not if
>   It be as short as yours.

In MS the sonnet bears the title 'En la muerte de Doña Guiomar de Sá Mujer de Juan Fernández de Espinosa'. According to Dámaso Alonso, to whose work the glossary that follows is greatly indebted, it can be inferred from her name that this lady was Portuguese; her father was Spanish (*el patrio Betis*) and her mother Portuguese (*el materno Tejo*, i.e. Tajo).

To its own element: the earth.
thorny: Góngora is playing on the lady's name *Espinosa* which literally means 'thorny'.
once it was on bush: when the lady was alive and married to Espinosa.
the sun's glory: her physical beauty.
the air's caress: her moral fragrance.
Faded ...: although the lady's body has perished, her soul continues to diffuse the moral fragrance of her good life.
Betis: the river Betis laments her deceased body (*its lovely leaves*) but not the continuing beauty of her soul (*its scent*); and even the lady's physical remains are gilded by the golden sands of the Tajo.
In other fields: in heaven.
a loftier dawn: of heavenly glory.
drops of dew: the dewdrops of this heavenly dawn are stars.

XXII On the baroque monument which Córdoba erected in honour of Queen Margaret of Austria, wife of Philip III, who died in 1611.

R.O. Jones, in his *Poems of Góngora* (Cambridge 1966), provides the following helpful *schema* for this difficult sonnet:

> The *túmulo*, an unmoving symbol of mutability,   A
> is the pyre (suggested by the candles) of a better
>   Phoenix.   B

>   It is like a ship assured of divine favour by
>   St Elmo's fire; its lights make it, through a
>   paradox, into a lighthouse beckoning to harbour.
>   Hence it stands for both stillness and
>   movement.   A¹
>   It is a shell from which the Queen will be reborn
>   into a new life (like the Phoenix from its pyre). B¹

St Elmo's fire and the myth of the Dioscuri refer to the same belief: that this phenomenon presaged a safe landing.

The Dioscuri were pictured with a star on their foreheads. If Góngora means the taper and candle lights of the catafalque, these (in Christian terms) may claim as their mother (*a better Leda*) Heaven's triumphant church. Or Góngora may be punning on the liturgical response 'May perpetual light shine upon her'.

Funeral machine: an elaborate and temporary monumental contrivance, like an enormous stage prop, erected inside the church; it did not contain the corpse.
a pearl's: the pun here, not renderable I think in English, is that Margarita, the lady's name, is also the Latin for 'pearl'.

XXIII   An inscription for the tomb of Domínico Greco (1545–1614).

key: the tomb is the key that locks him in death.
The Greek ... etc: Salcedo, quoted by Dámaso Alonso, glosses these lines as follows: 'By his death [El Greco's] Nature inherited his most perfect works of art; Art inherited his studious application to perfect itself; Iris inherited his colours to be her greatest ornament; Phoebus his lights to shine more resplendently; and Morpheus his shades with which to show his terrors. He beseeches common feeling to soften with its tears the marble that entombs him, and to offer him the balm of feeling and precious aroma.'

XXIV   On the death of Henry IV, King of France. Henry was stabbed by the mad priest Ravaillac on May 14, 1610.

XXV   'Royal Saint Lawrence of the Escorial' is the subject of the poem.

The pinnacles of the Escorial, in their height and splendour, blot out the brilliance of the sun-reddened clouds; and Heaven dreads them as more terrible giants than those who once warred against it.

Jupiter may lay aside his bolts since these pinnacles are not new giants; and the Sun need not fear to show its rays since the beams of these pinnacles are lanterns to a church which was raised by Spain's greatest King, Philip II, to Spain's greatest Martyr, San Lorenzo.

Philip II, conqueror of the New World, the Philippines and other archipelagoes.

the Parcae: the Fates.

XXVI   To the Conde de Villamediana, celebrating the pleasure he derived from diamonds, paintings and horses.

In Góngora's time some connoisseurs had precious stones set in lead to emphasize their qualities by contrast. Góngora's rich and extravagant friend, Villamediana, seems to have indulged in this fashion.

The stones which the East denies to others (who have not the wealth to buy nor the taste to enjoy them), even in an uncut state and not set in gold but in base lead, compete with the sun in splendour.

Villamediana's private picture gallery contains paintings by Spanish and foreign masters; so skilfully executed are these works that they can speak, in the aesthetics of colour, if not actually.

Andalusian horses were renowned for their swiftness. The mares conceive by the wind: they are in heat 'when ... winnowed chaff by western winds is blown'; thus in Dryden's *Georgics* (III).

XXVII   The mountain referred to is the Guadarrama. The would-be Viceroy of Naples (1610–1616), the Count of

Lemos, Góngora's patron, was a *Castro*, hence *Caistro*; his consort was a *Silva*, hence *Silvia*: both are hispanized from Vergil's *Aeneid* I.495 and VII.503.

XXVIII As Dámaso Alonso has remarked, Góngora wrote this sonnet in reply to some ladies at Vallodolid, who did not favour Andalusian gentlemen.

Andalusians carry off the prize for both gallantry and courage.

XXIX To Córdoba. This poem was written by Góngora on the occasion of a sojourn in Granada ('Those ruins and spoils enriched / By Genil, lapped by Dauro'): the sting here is that Granada is no beauty of a city in comparison with Góngora's beloved Córdoba.

No doubt Góngora had in mind Psalm 137: 'If I forget thee, O Jerusalem, let my right hand forget her cunning. If I do not remember thee, let my tongue cleave to the roof of my mouth; if I prefer not Jerusalem above my chief joy.'

Great river: the Guadalquivir.

XXXII This is one of three sonnets on the tomb of Queen Margarita. M. Artigas says of this tomb: 'Blas de Marabel, senior master of buildings [in Córdoba] ... built a bizarre and majestic tomb which was a cause of pride for the Cordobans. Large cards with Latin and Spanish poetry adorned the tomb.' (For the tomb, see the note on XXII above.)

The comparison is with a plume of feathers held and weighted in a precious stone.

despondent though bright spire: the tomb had a pyramid shape and was lit up with candles.
wise: recognizing the vanity of human pomp, these eyes must now see the truth and weep.
your hundred eyes: human ambition is compared with the peacock's tail; according to Greek myth, Juno transferred the hundred eyes of the slain Argus to the peacock's tail, a bird sacred to her.

XXXIII Without his patrons and protectors, Góngora looks to a bleak future.

an ilex tree: symbol of Rodrigo Calderón, Góngora's protector; losing royal favour, he was executed on October 21, 1621.

a laurel: Juan de Tasis, Conde de Villamediana, was assassinated on August 21, 1622, allegedly for courting Queen Isabel de Borbón in a poem (hence the reference to Calliope).

Minerva's learnèd tree: the olive. Pedro Fernández de Castro, Conde de Lemos, died on October 19, 1622, having fallen from royal favour some time before this.

XXXIV   It seems that the lady was born somewhere between Soria and Porto, along the course of the Duero. Curiously, this is also the location of Jorge de Montemayor's *Diana* (1542).

noble cot: the lady was of noble birth.
a half-moon: Cupid's bow.
the chaste huntress: Artemis or Diana, goddess of hunting; represented with a bent bow and a quiver; supposed to be the same as the moon.
Eurotas: a river in Sparta; laurels, myrtles and olives grew plentifully on its banks.
she points two: since there was a likelihood of a single love-arrow falling out, Ovid gave Cupid two arrows, a gold-tipped to arouse, and a leaden one to depress. (*Metamorphoses* I.447 ff.)

XXXVI   *its nine lights*: a reference to the Ariadne constellation.

XXXVIII   In considering this sonnet, Dámaso Alonso draws attention to its finely calculated pauses. Characteristically, the poem is an elaboration of a simple mishap into a grand baroque design culminating in the almost Chinese final line.

    The scansion of lines 3, 5, 7, 9 and 13 requires poetic licence: no fewer than seven diphthongs must be disjointed: *di-amante, ingeni-osamente, apremi-ado, impaci-ente, insidi-oso, indi-ano, invidi-osa*. It cannot be casual.

jointed nacre: the finger.
jail: the ring.
diamond: the diamond, like the ring, is imprisoned.
brave, impatient: Clori is not only patient, she is also brave, *gallarda*; Góngora, with fine miniaturist skill, is playing with chivalric convention.

XXXIX The cataclysm of Góngora's poem belongs to the order of the literary imagination. Nonetheless, as Dámaso Alonso has pointed out, the world here is very different from the delightful world (*el lugar ameno*) of the Renaissance. Here is a powerful and succinct expression of the 'shudder of the baroque'. The Góngora poem will doubtless remind readers of English poetry of Donne's equally powerful poem:

> At the round earth's imagin'd corners, blow
> Your trumpets, Angells, and arise, arise
> From Death, you numberlesse infinities
> Of Soules, and to your scattred bodies goe,
> All whom the flood did, and fire shall o'er throw.

The essential difference between the two poems can be seen in the last line of Góngora's: while Donne's vision is relentlessly terrible, Góngora's unexpected conclusion in *cuidados* obliges the reader to consider the poem's vision of anarchy as a *device*. Góngora's Day of Judgment, while biblical in its sources, is accommodated or tamed by literature. It is the writer in Góngora, not the priest, who predominates in the poem.

bolting winds: the verb *desbocarse* is used in referring to horses racing out of control.
kiss: here *besar* has the force of 'bite' (as in the colloquial Americanism, 'to bite the dust').
spew up: as do volcanoes.
forded ill by thoughts: not even the imagination dares to cross over these currents.
days of Noah: the forty days of the Flood.
cares: *cuidados*, 'love's anxieties'.

XL The personal background to this sonnet is a journey made by Góngora in 1593 to Salamanca where he fell seriously ill.

Characteristically of Góngora, the sexuality of the poem's ermine-clad lady, momentarily Ovidian, is finally contained in the neat verbal gesture of the last tercet. Góngora prefers his eroticism – if one may use such a strong term – at as many removes as he can manage with his immense skills of suggestion and allusion, and this is certainly one function of his *culteranismo*.

XLIII If the beauty of the young girl could cast a powerful spell on the poet, what resistance can he now offer to her mature beauty?

undressed yet armed (line 3): Cupid, represented as a winged infant, armed with a bow and a quiver full of arrows.
line 5: the temptation of passion.
lilies ... violets (lines 5 and 6): the grown woman and the girl she once was.
lines 7 and 8: in her youth, the lady already possessed the beauty of her maturity.
saddened voice (line 9): Góngora cannot allow himself to yield to passion, but can only sing of it like the nightingale.
lines 14 and 15: like dawn, the beauty of the lady will start a dawn chorus.

XLIV The basic situation of the poem, the barely perceptible infrastructure on which Góngora has built his architectonic fantasy of baroque conceit, is that of unrequited love. But the very manifestation of the poet's grief, his tears and sighs, is obliterated, as if conspiratorially, by the wind and the trees. Thus, the fiercely *human* angel, the beloved, will not even be aware of the misery she has caused. Not only is the poet's love unrequited, but there is the further and therefore more anguished frustration of its expression being ineffectual.

Alcides: a surname of Minerva in Macedonia. She was goddess of wisdom, war and all the liberal arts; the olive tree was sacred to her. Elsewhere in Góngora, the olive tree alludes, by virtue of its grey and green leaves, to age.
that fiercely human angel: the lady of the poem.

XLV *Strymo*: river of Thrace; the reference is to Orpheus.

XLVI *great lord*: Neptune.

XLVII Góngora draws an analogy between his own fate in love and the fate of Phaëton. He beseeches the poplars, once Phaëton's sisters, to mourn his misfortune in love as they once lamented the fall of their brother.

Phaëton was a son of the sun, of Phoebus and Clymene. He was a lively, handsome figure with whom Venus fell in love. Consequently he became vain and ambitious and when Epaphus, the son of Io, told him to check his pride and denied his paternity, Phaëton decided to visit Phoebus and make him declare his legitimacy. Under pressure, Phoebus swore that he would grant him any request and Phaëton demanded to be allowed to drive Phoebus' chariot for one day. Reluctantly, Phoebus granted him his request.

Phaëton, however, paid little or no attention to the instructions he was given and failed to keep the horses of the sun on their right course, thus threatening the world with incineration. Seeing this, Jupiter struck Phaëton down with a bolt and he fell into the river Po. His burnt body was found by the nymphs and decently buried. His sisters, grieving his death, were turned by Jupiter into poplars.

XLVIII A moral warning to the middle-aged?

Blind human reason: man is blind in that he cannot achieve morally (rejuvenation) what the snake accomplishes physically.
heavy share: the body.
sovereign sapphire: heaven.
light self: the soul.

XLIX Góngora masterfully applies his technical skills to give his treatment of the *carpe diem* theme some novelty by correlation. The hair of youth is gold; the neck crystal; the lip a pink carnation; the forehead a lily. The gold of the hair turns to silver; the pink carnation of the lip turns to lopped pansy; the gold, crystal, carnation and lily of beauty turn to clay, smoke, dust and shadow; all of which together turn to nothing, the physical obliteration of death.

Professor R.O. Jones writes of this sonnet: 'The poetic injunction to a young girl to enjoy her youth and beauty while they last – Ausonius' *collige, virgo, rosas* – was a stock subject for imitating in the Renaissance. It is a commonplace to compare Góngora's sonnet with Garcilaso's on the same theme, "En tanto que de rosa y azucena". Góngora's sonnet is different from its models, however: it warns not of the coming of old age but of extinction. Garcilaso's sonnet retains its luminous poise and measure to the end; the last line of Góngora's is a personal cry of horror at the thought of ceasing to exist.'

LI The occasion of the poem was the operation of bloodletting on a lady's foot.

the mournful fate of her: Eurydice, wife of the singer poet Orpheus; fleeing from an over-zealous lover, she was bitten by a serpent in the grass and died of the venomous bite.

Appendices

Góngora's Defence of Poetic Obscurity: text from José María Valverde, *El barroco. Una visión de conjunto*, Montesinos Editor, Barcelona 1983, p. 52.

For a black lady's sake . . . : this *romance* was attributed to Góngora in 1903 by Adolfo de Castro. The poem seems to me so characteristic of the master in its poise and inventiveness that, if not written by him, then it was written by a reincarnation.

Index of Spanish First Lines

Al tramontar del sol, la ninfa mía, 108
Al tronco descansaba de una encina, 102
Amarrado al duro banco, 24
Aprended, flores, en mí, 40
¡Ayer deidad humana, hoy poca tierra, 76

Caído se le ha un clavel, 18
Cosas, Celalba mía, he visto extrañas, 114
Cristales el Po desata, 50
Cual parece al romper de la mañana, 106

De la florida falda, 48
De pura honestidad templo sagrado, 70
Descaminado, enfermo, peregrino, 116

El Cuarto Enrico yace malherido, 84
En dos lucientes estrellas, 62
En el cristal de tu divina mano, 110
En este occidental, en este, oh Licio, 132
En tenebrosa noche, en mar airado, 72
Esta en forma elegante, oh peregrino, 82
Este monte, de cruces coronado, 74

Gallardas plantas, que con voz doliente, 130

Herido el blanco pie del hierro breve, 138
Hermana Marica, 52
Hermosas damas, si la pasión ciega, 92

La dulce boca que a gustar convida, 120
La más bella niña, 32
La mitad del alma, 64
Las flores del romero, 36
Las que a otros negó piedras Oriente, 88
Lloraba la niña, 28

Máquina funeral, que desta vida, 80
Mátanme los celos, 64
Menos solicitó veloz saeta, 136
Mientras por competir con tu cabello, 134
Montaña inaccesible, opuesta en vano, 90

Ni en este monte, este aire, ni este río, 126
No de fino diamante o rubí ardiente, 100
No son todos ruiseñores, 44

¡Oh claro honor del líquido elemento, 128
¡Oh excelso muro, oh torres coronadas, 94
¡Oh niebla del estado más sereno, 96
Oveja perdida, ven, 22

Pálida restituye a su elemento, 78
Pender de un leño, traspasado el pecho, 66
Perdí la esperanza, 64
Por una negra señora, 144
Prisión del nácar era articulado, 112

¡Que se nos va la Pascua, mozas, 58

Sacros, altos, dorados chapiteles, 86
Si Amor entre las plumas de su nido, 122
Si ociosa no, asistió naturaleza, 68
Suspiros tristes, lágrimas cansadas, 124

Verdes juncos del Duero a mi pastora, 104

Ya besando unas manos cristalinas, 98
Yacen aquí los huesos sepultados, 118

POETICA

APOLLINAIRE: Selected Poems
Oliver Bernard

FLOWER AND SONG (Aztec Poems)
Edward Kissam and Michael Schmidt

HÖLDERLIN: Poems and Fragments
Michael Hamburger

POEMS OF JULES LAFORGUE
Peter Dale

THE LAMENTATION OF THE DEAD
Peter Levi

LI HE: Goddesses, Ghosts, and Demons
J. D. Frodsham

MARTIAL: Letter to Juvenal
Peter Whigham

THE POEMS OF MELEAGER
Peter Whigham and Peter Jay

GÉRARD DE NERVAL: The Chimeras
Peter Jay and Richard Holmes

NIETZSCHE: Dithyrambs of Dionysus
R. J. Hollingdale

THE NOISE MADE BY POEMS
Peter Levi

OLD ENGLISH RIDDLES
Michael Alexander

PALLADAS: Poems
Tony Harrison

THE SATIRES OF PERSIUS
W.S. Merwin

AN UNOFFICIAL RILKE (Poems 1912–1926)
Michael Hamburger

RIMBAUD: A Season in Hell and Other Poems
Norman Cameron

SLOW CHRYSANTHEMUMS
(Classical Korean Poetry in Chinese)
Kim Jong-gil

THE SELECTED POEMS OF TU FU
David Hinton